Who is my neighbour?

Report on an Ecumenical Visit to the Middle East

10-24 March 2001

CHURCHES TOGETHER
IN BRITAIN AND IRELAND

Published by:
Churches Together in Britain and Ireland
Inter Church House 35-41 Lower Marsh
London SE1 7SA

+44 (0)20 7523 2121 fax +44 (0)20 7928 0010
global@ctbi.org.uk
www.ctbi.org.uk

registered charity number 259688
ISBN number: 0 85169 263 X

Cover picture "Via Dolorosa" - Christian Aid
printed by DAP (Sussex) Ltd

Contents

Foreword

This book is about a number of ecumenical journeys in the Middle East made over a two-week period in March 2001. It records a range of voices from Israel, Palestine and their neighbours. The range is not entirely comprehensive – the spectrum is so wide – so there are no Muslim Brothers nor Hamas, no Zionist Settlers nor Millennial Dispensationalists. There is still a range, facilitated by ecumenical contacts in the region, which enable some of the important realities of the Middle East, political and religious, to be articulated. It is the hope that this report will enable them to be heard widely within the British and Irish churches, if not beyond, and encourage further contact with the peoples of the region.

Twenty years ago an ecumenical delegation visited the Middle East on behalf of the British Council of Churches. Its report was entitled *Towards Understanding the Arab-Israeli Conflict.* In 1989 another BCC delegation visited Israel and the Occupied Territories. Its report was entitled *Impressions of Intifada.*

The choosing of a title for this document has been an interestingly difficult task. Given the centrality of the Israel-Palestine crisis it was tempting to find inspiration in a poignant, haunting cry heard several times, in Gaza, and Jerusalem, the shortest version of which was, "Delegations Come, Delegations Go, Nothing Ever Changes". On balance, however, we felt that the title should reflect the initial vision of the visit, that it be to "the Middle East" and not just to Israel and the Occupied Territories. The title therefore needed, if possible, to be regionally-relevant, thought-provoking and immediately to the point.

Who is my neighbour? goes theologically to the heart of the crisis in Middle East. Behind the violence and the strident politics there is this primary insistent question, a recognizable gift of the region's Christian heritage – for Arabs and non-Arabs, Christians, Jews and Muslims.

Acknowledgements are due to all the members of the CTBI delegation, without whose writings this report would have been impossible to compile. David Fong and Anne van Staveren, CTBI colleagues, need to be thanked for their support in the briefing and editing processes. Above all, many thanks are due to friends in the Middle East, within and outside the structures of the Middle East Council of Churches, without whose active cooperation this visit would not have taken place. Any errors of fact or perception are solely the responsibility of the CTBI group.

Paul Renshaw *CTBI Coordinating Secretary for International Affairs*
July 2001

Executive Summary

The Middle East exercises a unique grip on world affairs through its very potent mix of religious, historical, economic and political influences. The impact on the region of the old imperial powers - Britain, France - is still felt. The sway exercised by the global superpower, the USA, is even stronger, through subventions to friendly Arab governments (Egypt, Jordan) and the maintenance of military bases (in the Gulf) to its decades-long support of the "State of the Jewish People" on virtually an "Israel, right or wrong" basis.

The Israel-Palestine and Iraq crises are two of the most contentious and current of foreign policy debates. Within the region they are seen as being linked together, providing evidence of "double standards" in the way the West enforces UN resolutions and imposes sanctions on Iraq but not on Israel. Christians in the region find their loyalty questioned in view of the actions of so-called "Christian" nations like the USA and UK. The perception of many Christians in the Middle East is that British and Irish churches support Israel and the continued bombing of Iraq.

Christianity was, until the Arab conquests of the seventh century, the dominant religious force in the region. By and large (Lebanon being the exception) Christians have for long had to live as a small minority, with all that that has meant in an Islamic milieu. The continuing existence of Christianity in some parts of the Middle East is today under greater threat than ever, mainly on account of emigration. Church leaders in Jerusalem are fearful that the "Holy Places" may become little more than a museum of Christianity within a generation if a just peace between Israelis and Palestinians cannot soon be found, the economy restored and emigration reversed. The consequences of Christian emigration are also of concern to the churches in Jordan and Lebanon.

These issues provided some of the context for the CTBI Ecumenical Visit to the Middle East which took place over a two-week period in mid-March 2001. It was the first such wide-ranging visit for nearly 20 years. A more focussed ecumenical visit to Israel and the Occupied Territories took place in 1989. Representatives of nine of CTBI's 33 member churches formed a twelve-strong delegation which, in the first week, split into two groups - visiting Lebanon and Syria, and Egypt and Jordan. The second week saw the delegation united for three days in Jerusalem before dividing again to visit Gaza, Galilee and the West Bank. On reconvening in Jerusalem the delegation reflected on their visit and issued a 16-point set of "Preliminary Reflections".

The visit was organized in close cooperation with staff of, and others associated with, the Middle East Council of Churches in all the countries visited. MECC acts as the regional ecumenical body which draws together the highly diverse nature of Middle Eastern Christianity through its "four family" structure - Oriental Orthodox, Eastern Orthodox, Catholic and Evangelical (Protestant).

The planned itineraries were very largely fulfilled, despite the uncertainties which entering Israel even in March entailed. Only a few days after the visit took place the Israel-Palestine crisis spiralled further downwards and it can now be said that the visit happened in a lull before the latest storm.

The range of contacts made by the delegation is given in the Itineraries (Appendix 1), but included figures from many levels in the religious world of the countries visited, senior politicians and their advisers, diplomats and workers in the fields of development, human rights and refugees.

The visit was intentionally to the Middle East and not just to Israel and the Occupied Territories. Middle Eastern Christianity often feels overlooked and forgotten in the West. One purpose of the visit was to help to negate that impression and to open British and Irish churches up to the possibility of identifying new ways of relating ecumenically to the region.

In visiting Israel's Arab neighbours the intention was also to look at the situation of Palestinian refugees and the impact of the Al-Aqsa Intifada on pan-Arab consciousness below the level of Government. While differences of political rhetoric between, say, Egypt and Syria are still clearly articulated, the question of "Zionism" remains a fundamental problem for many in the Arab Middle East.

The visit to the Middle East took place soon after Ariel Sharon became Prime Minister of Israel. If he was elected by a nation in shock, at the collapse of the Camp David talks (August 2000) and outbreak of the Intifada, the fact of his election was a shock for the Arab world, felt nowhere more keenly than in Lebanon, as some of the delegation heard from the Prime Minister. Exposure to long-term Palestinian refugees in Beirut and Amman, in Gaza and Bethlehem, and witnessing the impact of Israel's "security" measures and its creation of "facts on the ground" (settlements, by-pass roads) in the Occupied Territories, illustrated some of the catastrophic, life-denying realities which Palestinians, Christian and Muslim, face on a daily basis. Meeting with people who inhabit high-level political corridors illuminated the depth of the chasm of mistrust and divergence of narrative between Israeli and Palestinian that perhaps diplomacy alone cannot bridge. The critical role of Christians able to speak the language of "reconciliation" was affirmed from outside the Christian fold.

The delegation returned aware that many of the basic issues identified in 1981 and 1989 remain to the solved. No wonder one of the most poignant phrases which returned to Britain and Ireland with the CTBI team was, "Delegations come, delegations go, nothing ever changes".

For that challenge to be answered the CTBI membership is asked to reflect on how it engages with the Middle East - in advocacy, mission support, prayer. "End the Occupation" is recognized as a key demand of Palestinian church leaders, among many others. Support for a return to negotiation based on international law is one of a number of perspectives to which CTBI churches are asked to give their assent. Continuing support for Jerusalem as "one city for two peoples and three faiths" is also commended.

New ways of relating ecumenically to the Middle East are also suggested, in particular the exploration of new links being made with the churches in Syria. The question of how denominational bodies which relate to parts of the Middle East can take on an ecumenical communications responsibility is also put forward for discussion.

Chapter 1

Why visit the Middle East?

1.　Background

The Ecumenical Visit to the Middle East in March 2001 was the first from Britain and Ireland for nearly 20 years. Given the political footprints which Britain has left in the region this might be thought surprising. Church-wise, however, there are relatively few direct "mission links" with Middle Eastern Christianity through which broad ranging contact can be naturally maintained. There have, of course, been many church-related visits to the Holy Land, at all kinds of levels, but the only other national ecumenical visit since 1981 was paid in 1989, to Israel and the Occupied Territories, provoked by what can now be seen to have been the first Palestinian Intifada.

Reports emanated from both these visits. Given the intractable nature of the Israel-Palestine problem these documents of yesteryear regrettably have present-day resonance, and were useful in providing reference points along our way.

2.　Genesis

The genesis for this visit lies in the seventh Assembly of the Middle East Council of Churches which took place in the Lebanon in May 1999, the first time it had been able to be held there for many years on account of the civil war. At such four-yearly occasions representatives of the four "families" of MECC member churches meet to express their ecumenical relationships - the Eastern (Byzantine) Orthodox, the Oriental Orthodox, the Catholics and the "Evangelicals" (in western terms a grouping of Protestants and some Evangelicals). Reports were made of various ecumenical visits to the region since the previous Assembly, which only pointed up the lack of British and Irish ecumenical contact. That was the context in which the idea of an Ecumenical Visit to the Middle East was hatched and subsequently proposed to and agreed by the CTBI Church Representatives' Meeting.

3.　Rationale

Britain has played a singular role in shaping the political landscape of the Middle East. The influence of Zionist-inclined leaders such as Lloyd George, Balfour and Churchill, the dilemmas it faced in managing its League of Nations Mandate over Palestine and final succumbing to American pro-Zionist pressure in the immediate post-war period contributed significantly to the direction and outcome of the clash between Zionists and Arabs over Palestine which began in the mid-nineteenth century.

Throughout the 1990s at the geo-political level Britain (with European Union partners) was largely content to play second fiddle while the USA tried to orchestrate a more harmonious tune between Israel and the Palestinians. Over Iraq, however, to the dismay of many British Christians and anger of Middle Eastern ones Britain played the role of "repetiteur" while the USA ploughed on through the score marked "Containment of Saddam".

The enduring religious significance of the region as the cradle of Christianity would hardly need mentioning except for the paradoxical fact that the Middle Eastern churches feel unrecognized and misunderstood outside the region as they battle with the implications of their minority status and their daily encounter with people of the two other Abrahamic faiths. The churches of the Middle East look for signs of recognition and support in their beleaguered situation. The visit was therefore primarily one of solidarity to the Christian churches within Israel-Palestine and the neighbouring states.

4.   Pattern of the visit
In trying to address the *regional* dimension the group needed to be split for part of their two weeks in the Middle East. The first week originally saw three teams going - to Beirut/Damascus, Cairo/Amman and Baghdad/Basra - before coming together in Amman and travelling together overland to Jerusalem.

In the second week, in Israel-Palestine, the visit envisaged three days together in Jerusalem before splitting into groups for two-day visits to Gaza, Galilee and the West Bank, depending on the situation on the ground at the time, before reconvening for final consultations and reflection.

5.   Timing
The timing of the visit was related in the first instance to avoiding the Millennial year, when potential partners in Israel-Palestine were likely to have their hands very full with visitors of all kinds. The first half of 2001 allowed some slippage in the Middle East Peace Process (MEPP) timetable, but did not foreshadow its collapse. It was believed all along that the visit would not be affected by the timetable of the MEPP, though its context and content would be. It turned out that, with the collapse of the MEPP at Camp David in August 2000 and the outbreak of the Second (Al-Aqsa) Intifada in September that some of these assumptions were not entirely valid. All the same the visit to Israel-Palestine proceeded according to plan. The planned visit to Iraq had to be abandoned near departure time when visas

approved by the Foreign Ministry in Baghdad were not made available in Amman. It remains a moot point as to whether this was done for political or other reasons. When the CTBI party returned home invitations awaited the original Iraq-bound group to a Churches' Conference in Baghdad in May. With the abandonment of Iraq in this instance, the group visiting Beirut was augmented.

6.   Contexts - regional and national

The visit took place against a background of several interlocking political contexts:

6.1   The deep "post-Oslo" crisis between "Israel" and "Palestine", its implications for peace-building between the two peoples and for relationships throughout and beyond the region, both religious and political, the role of the USA and that of the EU. There was uncertainty at the time of the visit about whether circumstances within Israel-Palestine would allow the whole programme to be implemented. In the end the CTBI visit ended four days before the crisis entered a new phase on 28 March. It has since become clear that the visit took place in a relative lull before an even fiercer storm.

6.2   The attempt by the Lebanon to consolidate the post-civil war peace and build a plural society, where the fragility of the ethnic/religious balance is felt to require the denial of citizenship to Palestinian (mainly Muslim) refugees.[1] Lebanon is struggling to rediscover the path to prosperity and national reconciliation in a context of an imperfect peace, neither geographically in the south nor "spiritually" as long as Syrian forces stay.

6.3   The implications of the post-Hafez Assad period in Syria, a country perhaps perched on the edge of modernizing change. Syria's self-perception is as a regional power with a long-term horizon in view. It sees its presence in Lebanon, not least in the Bekaa valley, in strategic terms as long as Israel remains perceived as a military threat. Syria exercises a capacity for independent action as seen in its recently agreed free trade agreement with Iraq.

6.4   Jordan in the early years of the Hashemite King Abdullah's reign, a country whose population is 40 per cent Palestinian, where subventions from the West remain critical to its well-being. Jordan needs good relations with Iraq and Syria as well as Israel. Like Egypt, Jordan is the signatory of a peace agreement with Israel, though its religious and political demography renders it more

---

1 The number of Palestinian refugees in Lebanon is both unclear and open to dispute. This is altogether a very "political" issue. The UN Relief and Works agency uses a figure of 370,000 for registered refugees. There are likely to be others who are unregistered. Some observers have, however, made lower estimates.

susceptible to upheaval in the event of a prolonged delay in the achievement of a plausible statehood by the Palestinians. Those risks have heightened since the visit.

6.5   Egypt, the political giant of the region, whose sense of "statehood" derives from antiquity, a country always in need of looking both south and east. Like Jordan, Egypt is the recipient of large amounts of American aid, a signatory to a peace treaty with Israel and committed to a non-violent, just resolution of the Israel-Palestine problem. Egypt's unique standing in the Arab world means that it is still a critical potential mediating body but its internal politics are not immune to the impact of a greatly prolonged search for peace between the Israelis and Palestinians.

6.6   Iraq, not being visited but "politically present" in that Saddam Hussein is re-establishing relationships within the Arab world, the credibility of the UN sanctions policy is at a low ebb and the USA and UK are isolated in their maintenance by air patrols of the so-called "No Fly Zones" over northern and southern Iraq, and young Palestinians are investing Saddam with hero status over against Yasser Arafat.

6.7   The Palestinians' need for a short-term cutting through of the Gordian knot of Middle East politics to secure a just peace with Israel on the basis of a two-state solution, the subsequent negotiation of a "return of refugees" process and the recovery of the Palestinian economy. On the other hand there are factors such as the weakness of the Palestinian Authority in maintaining itself organizationally, the uncertainty about its future leadership, direction and legitimacy and relations with avowedly Islamist bodies such as Hamas.

6.8   The variegated, highly fragmented Israeli Jewish political scene - from the Haredim for whom the State of Israel is a religious irrelevance before the coming of the Messiah, through Biblical Zionists who see Judaea and Samaria (which includes the West Bank) as God's inalienable gift to the Jewish people, to those who say that "the land does not belong to us, we belong to the land". In the midst is the military mind-set of the "securocrats", led by Ariel Sharon, which tends to equate "Palestinian" with "terrorist" and, ten years after the first Intifada, still take "security measures" which the international community considers excessive and disproportionate if not beyond the pale.

7.   Dimensions to the visit

7.1   The phrase "showing the flag" may not be the most apt, but there was something of that about it. The visit was one of demonstrating, through CTBI, an ecumenical concern for Middle East churches and their people, everywhere in small minorities, where the notion of "Christian Presence" carries the particular overtone of fear for the Church's future, perhaps especially critically in the land of Christ's birth.

7.2   A balance needed to be held between the "pastoral" and "political", recognizing that Christians in the Arab countries have their own issues to share which they do not want to be defined wholly in terms of what is going on in the land west of the Jordan. On the other hand, Jerusalem is a very special place for them, so the search for a "just peace" that will facilitate the lowering of barriers and promote regional contact is their interest too. The impact of the second Intifada on pan-Arab consciousness, not least in a time of satellite communication, was one new dimension for which the CTBI visitors sought to have sensitive ears.

7.3   Consulting with Christian leaders and representatives of other faith communities in Israel-Palestine on the future of peace-building in the wake of the advent of Ariel Sharon to the Premiership in Israel was a primary element in the visit. In this task the CTBI party bore in mind the Principles for engagement with the Middle East Peace Process advocated through CTBI for the last nearly five years (see page 25).

7.4   The deepening of understanding of Christian-Muslim relations in the different national contexts was an essential component, not least because it is a subject where stories of episodic violence and systemic discrimination carry both validity and partiality and thereby pose difficulties for interpretation. The very minority nature of Christianity can engender an insecurity which colours inter-religious relationships, however easy they may be.

7.5   The most critical qualification for participation in the visit was that of being a good listener. (It was an Irish speaker, significantly, who, at the Briefing Meeting held in February, said that the main task would be to "listen loudly" to the multi-layered dynamics of the Middle East).

8.   Anticipated outcomes
8.1   Enriched understanding that would support advocacy work of the churches together on issues of Middle East concern, whether it be in the area of inter faith relations, the future of Israel-Palestine, or (despite the lack of a visit) the question of sanctions on Iraq and regional security.
8.2   Recommendations to CTBI member churches on issues of the most pressing political nature concerning British, Irish and EU relations with the Middle East, especially Israel-Palestine.

8.3   The deepening of ecumenical relations in a way which will inform the work of the Middle East Forum (Churches' Commission on Mission) and possibly result in commending new ways of relating ecumenically to the Middle East.
8.4   Material for a report which will do justice to the investment in the visit.
8.5   The possibility of interest being expressed by Middle East churches in a return visit.

9.   Participants

A twelve-person delegation was identified between July and December 2000, drawn from nine member churches of CTBI and from all four nations. The nature of the agenda - and the rarity of the visit – meant that some pains were taken to secure the participation of a number of senior denominational figures. The final group of twelve included three women and ranged in age from early thirties to "third age". Two-thirds had previously visited the Middle East. The members were:

The Very Revd Dr Robert Davidson
Retired Professor of Old Testament Language and Literature in the University of Glasgow. Moderator (1990/91) of the General Assembly of the Church of Scotland. Representative of the Church of Scotland Moderator in the Presidency of the Council of Christians and Jews.

The Revd Frederick George*
Originally from Sri Lanka, Minister of a Baptist Church in north London. President (1998) of the Baptist Union of Great Britain.

The Revd Christopher Gillham
Minister of two Congregational Churches in west Wales. President (1998) of the Congregational Federation. Representative of Federation in contacts with Albania and Lebanon.

Esther Hookway
Oecumenical Patriarchate (Archdiocese of Thyateira and Great Britain). Formerly Project Coordinator and Youth Trainer for World Student Christian Federation-Europe and Syndesmos (World Fellowship of Orthodox Youth), now working with the Institute for Orthodox Christian Studies.

Gillian Kingston*
An Irish national, Methodist lay preacher. Moderator of the Church Representatives' Meeting of Churches Together in Britain and Ireland. Member of the Methodist /Roman Catholic International Commission.

14

The Rt Revd Michael Langrish*

Anglican Bishop of Exeter. Previously Suffragan Bishop of Birkenhead (1993-2000). Diocese linked with the Episcopal Diocese of Cyprus and the Gulf.

The Revd Sigrid Marten

Of German Lutheran origin, a Presbyterian parish minister in the inner city of Glasgow, Scotland. Since 1999 Convener of the International Interests Subcommittee of the Committee on Church and Nation of the Church of Scotland.

Dr Charles Reed

A former research consultant to the European Commission in Brussels, currently International Affairs Secretary of the Church of England (Anglican).

Paul Renshaw**

International Affairs Secretary of Churches Together in Britain and Ireland since 1998. Attended the MECC Assembly in the Lebanon (1999). Coordinator of the visit.

The Revd Hywel Wyn Richards*

Congregational minister of the Welsh-speaking Union of Welsh Independents with oversight of seven churches in North Wales; Chairman of UWI Christian Citizenship Committee.

The Revd Dr Frank Turner SJ

Assistant General Secretary of the Catholic Bishops' Conference of England and Wales, with overall staff responsibility for International Affairs. A member of a Caritas Europa delegation to Iraq in January 2001.

The Revd John Waller

Deputy General Secretary, United Reformed Church. Previously Moderator of the West Midlands Synod (1985-95).

*   members of the group who visited Egypt and Jordan.
**   started with the Lebanon group but then joined the Egypt group.

The others started the Middle East visit in Beirut.

Chapter 2

The Middle East – churches and ecumenism

The Christian population of the Middle East these days numbers no more than 15 million, a small minority in an environment which for centuries has been under hegemonic Islamic influences. The lives of Christians are set in the unique, very special region which gave birth to the Judaeo-Christian tradition itself. It was also in the Middle East that the early Christian controversies played themselves out and the first divisions in the Church occurred[2]. The history of the people and churches of the Middle East is fit for a truly multicoloured tapestry of very significant proportions.

1.   Middle East Council of Churches[3]

The relatively small number of Christians in the Middle East means that "people know each other, and there is a bond of kinship that is rather special" between them. It is no accident, therefore, that the Middle East Council of Churches chose to organize itself as a "family of families". "Each makes its contribution to the witness of all."

The MECC was established in May 1974, bringing together the Oriental and Eastern Orthodox families and the Evangelicals (Protestants) in one ecumenical body. It succeeded the Protestant churches' ecumenical instrument, the Near East Council of Churches (1962). At MECC's fifth General Assembly (1990) the seven Catholic churches of the Middle East joined the council as its fourth family. This symbolically completed "a square of wholeness, and made of the council a fully inclusive body".

The geo-political context places heavy burdens on MECC. In a region overwhelmingly Muslim in complexion, the MECC works quietly in a variety of ways, for example as an agent of mercy and reconciliation in war-torn Lebanon; interceding from time to time in the search for peace between Israel and the Palestinians, engaging in relief work in Iraq soon after the Gulf War, initiating inter faith discussions within Arab society in the examination of what should go into building a just and peaceful civil society.

---

2 A good web source on the early Ecumenical Councils is www.livingweb.com/library/270.htm

3 Main source for sections 1-5 is MECC's website, www.meccchurches.org

2.   Membership

MECC's "catchment area" stretches from Algeria to Iran, from Sudan to Cyprus. Its headquarters are in Beirut, having been re-established recently after a lengthy relocation to Cyprus on account of the Lebanese crisis. Regional offices are maintained in Cairo, Amman, Damascus, and Cyprus and a Liaison Office in the Gulf States. Currently its members are

The Oriental Orthodox Churches: (3)
* Armenian Apostolic Church, Catholicosate of Cilicia
* Coptic Orthodox Church
* Syrian Orthodox Church of Antioch and All the East

The Eastern (Byzantine) Orthodox Churches: (4)
Greek Orthodox Church of Alexandria and All Africa
* Greek Orthodox Church of Antioch and All the East
* Greek Orthodox Church of Jerusalem
Greek Orthodox Church of Cyprus

The Catholic Churches: (7)
Armenian Catholic Church of Cilicia
* Chaldean Catholic Church of Babylon
* Coptic Catholic Church of Alexandria
* Greek Catholic (Melkite) Patriarchate of Antioch, Alexandria and Jerusalem
* Latin Patriarchate of Jerusalem
* Maronite Church of Antioch
* Syrian Catholic Church of Antioch

The Evangelical Churches: (17)
* The Evangelical Church of Egypt (Synod of the Nile)
* The Episcopal Church in Jerusalem and the Middle East
* The Diocese of Egypt
* The Diocese of Jerusalem, Jordan, Syria and Lebanon
The Diocese of Cyprus and the Gulf
The Diocese of Iran
Episcopal Church in the Sudan
The Evangelical Church in Sudan
* Evangelical Lutheran Church in Jordan
The Synod of the Evangelical Church of Iran
* National Evangelical Synod of Syria and Lebanon
* The National Evangelical Union of Lebanon
The Presbyterian Church in the Sudan

The Union of the Armenian Evangelical Churches in the Near East
Protestant Church in Algeria
Eglise Reformée de France en Tunisie
The National Evangelical Church in Kuwait

(* = MECC member church which figured in the CTBI visit)

There remain, as MECC acknowledges, small Protestant churches in the region with links to non-ecumenical western churches and mission agencies. Dialogue with them (and with their partners) continues. Among the principal conciliar churches still not fully within the Middle Eastern ecumenical stream is the Ancient (Assyrian) Church of the East, the strongest Christian presence in Iraq.

3.   MECC's role

The MECC describes itself as "a meeting-place for the indigenous churches of the region, a facilitator of their common response to common needs". It encourages and supports relationships between its member churches in "an ecclesiastically sensitive manner, adhering to the historical confessions of the united Church, the Apostles' and Nicene Creeds, to which all its members subscribe. Its family structure emphasizes consensus and participation in community. Larger and smaller families each have equal opportunity to have their voices heard in its deliberations, and no one perspective is permitted to eclipse any other. The decision-making process of the MECC is sensitive to the various church traditions represented."

The Middle East Council of Churches thus sees itself as a fellowship of churches relating to the main stream of the modern ecumenical movement, the same which gave birth to the World Council of Churches and other regional ecumenical councils throughout the world.

4.   Five themes

Five key themes characterize the programme and activities of MECC:
1.   Strengthening a sense of unity, confidence, continuity and purpose within the fellowships of its member churches. Activities and programmes seek to encourage Christians to remain in the region and to make positive contributions towards its new and better future.

2.   Encouraging member churches to support and uphold each other as they help their people understand their faith and witness. "Within the MECC Christian dialogue takes place on all levels, from the pastoral grassroots to academic halls,

from formal dialogue among church leaders to the day-to-day fellowship among Christians on the street."

3.   Building bridges of understanding and mutual respect between Christians and people of other faiths. MECC "believes that Christians have a vital role to play within the Middle East's pluralistic society. Although numerically small, a self-confident and committed Christian community knows how to respect and celebrate diversity".

4.   Nurturing within the churches the spirit and resources for service (diakonia) in an arena replete with economic, political and often violent conflict.

5.   Mediating not only between Christians and churches in the Middle East, but also between them and their brothers and sisters in Christ elsewhere by seeking to overcome the "social and cultural gaps (which) often impede or undermine understanding".

5.   MECC churches and Middle East peace

Appendices 3, 4 and 5 are recent texts through which the leaders of the Middle Eastern churches express their perspectives on many of the issues which, in limited and various ways, the CTBI delegation encountered during its two-week visit. Within the diversity that is evident in these documents there are several unifying threads, e.g. ecumenical relationships, Christians' emigration from and Christian presence in the Middle East, Christian witness in an Islamic milieu, conflict and peacemaking in the Middle East. One of the strongest dimensions of the latter is summed up in the name "Israel".

The churches of the MECC family relate to the Israel-Palestinian crisis against the background of differing internal political contexts, both vis-à-vis Israel and in terms of local Christian-Muslim dynamics. At either end of a spectrum there stand Egypt and Syria, rivals for influence in the region - one having signed a peace treaty with Israel, the other not, one eschewing the language of war, the other not entirely. Neither country, in any case, is able to "take on" Israel in military terms.

Lebanon, of course, has its own singular diversity to manage in the aftermath of a civil war in which Israel was a potent factor for many years until very recently. Its Christian communities, some of which are part of church groupings which also cover Syria, are in complicated domestic situations. In Jordan the small Christian community has to take note of the political hand which the government has to play in balancing solidarity with the people of the West Bank (co-citizens until 1967) and Jordan's economic relationships with Iraq and Syria.

In the middle are the churches of the Holy Land, who have to cope on a daily basis with the tightening, life-denying impact of occupation on the lives of their congregations and their fellow Palestinians and to deal not in the language of rhetoric but in that of appeal to Christians the world over for support of spiritual and practical kinds. MECC resolutions, and statements between Assemblies, have regularly called for the rights of the Palestinian people, their Arab brothers and sisters, to self-determination to be respected and for the "Arab identity" of Jerusalem to be re-asserted in the face of its perceived "Judaisation" at the hands of the Israeli Government.

Chapter 3

CTBI churches and the Middle East

1. A backward glance

The Ecumenical Visit to the Middle East in 2001 lies within a stream of ecumenical concern for the region stretching back many years. CTBI's predecessor body, the British Council of Churches[4] (which, despite its name, also had Irish members) maintained two Advisory Committees on the Middle East, one reflecting the concerns of the missionary societies and the other those of the Division of International Affairs. In the 1970s the latter produced two study documents, *The Conflict in the Middle East and Religious Faith* (1970) and *Some Reflections on the Arab-Israeli Conflict* (1976).

2. BCC visit to the Middle East, 1981

In September 1981 the BCC sent a seven-member high-level delegation to the Middle East.[5] In a little under three weeks the delegation visited Lebanon, Syria, Jordan, Israel and the territories of the West Bank, Gaza and East Jerusalem and Egypt.

The purpose of the visit, largely organized by MECC, was
- to express the goodwill and fellowship of the Council and of the British and Irish churches to the peoples and governments of the area,
- to enter into the political predicaments of the area at the deepest possible level of understanding and prayer,
- to learn from and encourage those in all countries of the region who are working for understanding and reconciliation,
- on its return to help British and Irish Christians to a better grasp of the human problems of the area and the possibilities of conciliation or other constructive developments in the area.

The 1981 visit took place, of course, long before the words "peace process" became part of the Middle East lexicon. The Palestine Liberation Organisation was still largely unrecognized outside the Arab world and in exile (at the time being based in Beirut). The then Soviet Union still had influence in the region, mainly

---

4 The Roman Catholic Bishops' Conferences were not members of the BCC, though friendly relationships existed.
5 Catholic participation in the visit was provided by the Catholic Institute of International Relations.

through Syria. Iraq was being armed by the West and Iran was in the early years of the Khomeini-inspired Islamic revolution.

The delegation's 130pp. report, ***Towards Understanding the Arab-Israeli Conflict,*** was published in June 1982. By then the Middle East was again in crisis, Israel having just invaded Lebanon. Its conclusions are still worthy of reference, e.g.

- On the Middle East as a whole - it is a region of "resources, faiths, cultures and personalities, as well as political problems".
- On the fragility of political structures - this means that "armed force, legal or illegal, is near the surface in all these societies".
- On Israeli "security" needs - while acknowledging Israel's right under international law to exist, the report asked the question as to whether time was Israel's ally in view of the fact that "demographically and militarily the facts are changing in the Middle East".
- On Palestinian rights - a "chain of events in the twentieth century over which the Palestinians had little control made them its victims…a solution is required which will satisfy the conflicting claims of these two peoples to the same territory".
- On Christian Presence - "recognition by Western churches is sought by the indigenous churches of the region, both in terms of their primary task of living at peace within the Muslim majority and the dignity and sense of responsibility which their leaders must carry on behalf of the universal Church for the area in which God has placed them".
- On Western Christians' attitudes to Israel - "to absolutise the State of Israel with a theological rationale is both theologically unsound and politically unwise..it discourages the spirit of compromise which must prevail if the modern Israel is to have security, the Palestinian Arabs justice and the area peace."
- On possible ways forward - "During the 1970s a Palestinian position emerged which amounted to a willingness on their part to contemplate a two-state solution…which in our view has to be taken seriously, despite the fact that, in the face of Israeli refusal to make any concessions, Palestinian attitudes have hardened latterly."
- On American involvement - "the American relationship with Israel establishes the USA as the one outside power which might induce a more flexible attitude by Israel towards proposals for a settlement".
- On Europe's role - the 1980 Venice Declaration was seen by Arab countries as a sign "of European willingness to try to influence the USA to take another view of the Middle East conflict", even though the Israelis rejected it as being evidence of Europe's dependency on the Middle East for oil.

- On Britain's role - the report asked that "British assurance of long-term support for Israel ought now to be coupled with more evident signs of recognition of the justice of the Palestinian call for self-determination".

3.   BCC Visit to Israel and the Occupied Territories, 1989

In December 1987 the first Intifada began when, during a mass protest in Gaza against the killing of four men returning from work in Israel, four Palestinians began to throw stones at the Israeli occupying forces. Intifada means more like 'shaking off' than 'uprising'. The Palestinians were saying to the Israelis, "We don't want you occupying us!"

In March 1989 a ten-person BCC delegation visited Israel and the Occupied Territories at the invitation of MECC. *Impressions of Intifada* is its 40pp. report. Many of the issues remain central to the Palestinians' situation over ten years later:

- The impact on the Palestinian economy and the education of the youth.
- The pressure on Christians to emigrate.
- The denial of resources to and the infringement of the human rights of Arab Israelis.
- The imposition of curfews on Palestinian areas and the sealing off of entrances to refugee camps.
- Intimidation of Palestinian women by Israeli forces or Jewish vigilante patrols.
- Detention without charge as an Israeli response to demonstrations, the bulldozing or blowing up of homes where a resident has been arrested for stone-throwing or on a similar charge.
- The high number of teenagers or children among the Palestinian casualties
- The leading role being played in the Intifada by Palestinian women.
- The role of Muslim fundamentalism, then relatively minor except, perhaps, in Gaza
- The deep lack of confidence of Palestinians in Israeli law and its administration.
- The restrictions on movement of Palestinians both within Israel and the Occupied Territories.
- The presence of Jewish settlements on occupied land - and its effect on water resources.

With respect to the Israelis the report referred to
- The myth in Israeli society that they are the only civilized people in the region.

- The Israeli belief that the creation of the State of Israel had been a blessing to Palestinians.
- The Israelis' determined opposition to the Intifada based on the feeling that "for Israel there is no second chance".
- The lack of appropriate training and equipment for the combating of the Intifada.
- The lack of evidence for their accusations that Palestinians put children in the front rank of demonstrations to mask the snipers behind them.
- The unpopularity of serving against the Intifada within the Israeli Defence Force, some evidence of the beginning of resistance to military conscription and mothers organizing against the draft.
- The large proportion of Jewish immigrants with negligible experience of democratic institutions.
- The existence of an Israeli "peace movement" which sought to detach Israel's sense of destiny from the Zionist focus on land (and hence settlements) to a concept of shared community and common security.
- The apparent fact that Israeli outrage at their own Jewish history of persecution seems not to have developed into a universal abhorrence of persecution.
- The existence among them of either an ignorance of the extent of brutality that is being perpetrated in their name or a realisation that they cannot control it. "Either way the Israelis cannot forever get away with the present level of violence which they are using to quell the violence of the Intifada".

The Report of the 1989 visit listed 18 items in its concluding section on "What can the Churches DO?" These included:
- The promotion of prayer for peace with justice.
- What has since become known as "alternative pilgrimage".
- Raising awareness within the churches and outside of the realities of the situation.
- Organizing exchanges with Palestinian Christians.
- Exploring "theology of land" issues with special reference to Christian Zionism.
- The channelling of humanitarian aid through the work of Christian Aid, MECC and WCC.
- Alerting women to the potentially brutalising effect on Jewish young people of army service in the Occupied Territories and to the suffering of Palestinian mothers and children.

- Commending Her Majesty's Government for its support of an international conference and encouraging it to use its influence with the USA to expedite this.
- Commending Her Majesty's Government for its support of EEC economic assistance to the Palestinian community and encouraging it to use its influence to expand trading possibilities with Palestinians.
- Continuing as opportunity allows to press the Israeli authorities to exercise power responsibly, to recognize the representative role of the PLO and to accept the need for a negotiated settlement within an international context.

4.   Church responses within the 1990s

4.1   At the ecumenical level

In 1995 a consultation document *Towards Peace in the Holy Land: Western Church Responsibility to Palestinian Christianity on the Threshold of the New Millennium* was circulated to member churches for study and comment. Subsequently, at the Church Representatives' Meeting held on 20 November 1996, a shorter paper, *The Holy Land, the Peace Process and the British and Irish Churches: Principles for Response,* was adopted for the guidance of the churches.

Fundamental principles

1. Commitment to the Peace Process - recalling the late Prime Minister Rabin's words, *"enough of killing".* The conflict must be solved by negotiation, through a political process, and not through resort to violence and confrontation.
2. Commitment to dialogue between Jews, Muslims and Christians on what constitutes a peace with justice and guaranteed security for the Israeli and Palestinian communities. This concern must extend to the Palestinians who are citizens of Israel, those in Gaza and the West Bank and in the Palestinian diaspora.
3. Support for the Palestinian Christians and the churches of the Holy Land in their continuing presence and witness and their (and our) concern for peace with justice. The voice of the indigenous Christian communities must be heard, and the British and Irish churches must respond appropriately to their message as ecumenical partners through denominational and ecumenical links. Steps should be taken to raise awareness among Christians in Britain and Ireland of the life and witness of the indigenous Palestinian churches, for example through supporting and organizing "alternative tourism".
4. Acceptance that Jerusalem is *"a city for two peoples and three faiths"* (Latin Patriarch Michel Sabbah, MECC President, Jerusalem). It is a holy

city for the three main monotheistic faiths - Judaism, Christianity and Islam, and a city of definitive importance for two national communities, the Israelis and the Palestinians. Therefore there should be no unilateral attempts to "decide", pre-empt or impose the status of Jerusalem. Its status is defined by international law and long-standing agreements.

5.   Religious freedom, the right of access to places of worship, and the right to gather for worship must be ensured. This is vital for Christians and Muslims, resident in the West Bank who, because of the closures, are prevented from entering Jerusalem.

What mutual recognition requires of the Israeli and Palestinian communities:

6.   The need for both communities to avoid actions which are provocative to the other side. Rejection of a return to the politics of mutual negation which characterized the pre-Oslo period, whereby the demands of one side were unacceptable to the other.

7.   Recognition of the right of both communities to self-determination, security, international recognition and protection of human rights.

8.   The need to ensure that the Palestinian economy can function - through an end to closures and actions adversely affecting Palestinians' right to work.

What is required for the future of the Peace Process:

9.   Implementation of agreements already made since 1948, particularly those signed in the Peace Process and a return to the phased programme of agreements leading as soon as possible to real progress in Final Status talks including, inter alia, the rights of Palestinian refugees.

10.   An end to the building and expansion of settlements and a negotiated agreement on the future of existing settlements.

11.   International commitment to the Peace Process, which is not only a responsibility of the two central parties, the Israelis and Palestinians, but is an international agreement co-sponsored by the USA and Russia. Support for British and Irish government and European Union initiatives to support and encourage the Peace Process. This needs to include independent monitoring of implementation of progress.

12.   Support by the British and Irish Governments, the EU and the wider international community for the Palestinian economy through, for example, investment in infrastructure, joint ventures and employment, and income generating schemes.

4.2   At the church level

The manner in which any one CTBI church responded to such a document reflected a variety of factors, each with a differing degree of strength - its own ecclesiology, its mission history, the influence of priorities of a confessional family and/or the ecumenical movement and individual concerns of church leaders or those of other strategically-placed people at different levels within the church.

Three CTBI churches most clearly voiced their concern on the Holy Land through developing a considered position within a deliberative forum, be it bishops' conference or church assembly:

The official *Catholic* position on Jerusalem (as expressed by its bishops in England and Wales) emphasises its "unique significance" for Jews, Christians and Muslims, calls for Jerusalem to be a "universal symbol of fraternity and peace" and believes that this vision must be reflected in a final settlement of the status of the city. The Catholic Bishops' Conference of England and Wales participates in an international Vatican-led network monitoring development of the Middle East Peace Process.

The General Assembly of the *Church of Scotland* receives frequent reports on the Holy Land from its Church and Nation Committee and Board of World Mission. Its long presence in Jerusalem, Jaffa and Tiberias gives it special insight into the fears of the Jewish community, though not in recent years at the cost of neglecting the "living stones" through its partnership with the Episcopal Diocese of Jerusalem and support of the Sabeel Liberation Theology Centre.

The *United Reformed Church* Assembly has developed a response to Middle East issues not from a mission history background but through a combination of "ecumenical alerts" and internal pressures. The URC expressed itself most recently in the 1999 Assembly where the Palestinian Delegate-General to the United Kingdom was received as a platform speaker. A composite resolution was subsequently endorsed which included clauses on the "thrice holy city" of Jerusalem and the Middle East Peace Process within a regional setting.

Within the churches there are, however, many other levels of activity which enable Christian voices to speak, whether it be church committees or provincial synods. The engagement of diocesan leaders in England and Wales in the Holy Land is noteworthy, particularly in the Anglican family, as is the commitment of the URC at the level of Provincial Moderator.

4.3   At the church leader level

At the level of engagement by church leaders, irrespective of the church's history of passing resolutions, there is evidence of continuing deep concern for the lack of peace with justice in the Holy Land. Though the Church of England's General Synod has not responded institutionally to the "Holy Land" issues since before the Oslo Peace Process started and therefore not yet endorsed the 1998 Lambeth Conference resolution on Jerusalem, the Archbishop of Canterbury has, on more than one occasion, affirmed on behalf of the Anglican Communion the principle of "one city for two peoples and three faiths".[6]

When called upon, in March 1999, to respond to the Jerusalem Patriarchs' call for solidarity and protest over the Israeli policy towards the residency rights of Palestinians in East Jerusalem, the response from leading church figures in Britain and Ireland was swift. Only a few of these leaders, representing the great majority of CTBI member churches, had institutional backing in a formal way, but they had a sense of what justice required of them.

4.4   At church agency level

Christian Aid, of the three CTBI-related development agencies,[7] commits the most resources to the Middle East. Indeed, it has been working with partner organizations there since the 1950s, not least the Middle East Council of Churches. Currently, Christian Aid partners work in the Occupied Territories and Israel, Lebanon, Egypt and northern Iraq, disbursing about £900,000 annually. Health provision, agriculture and food security, empowering women and human rights are among the priorities of Christian Aid's partners.

Christian Aid's focus has broadened out in recent years from merely the funding of long-term development projects and emergencies. More specific attention is now given to the wider political, social and economic context in which poverty is rooted. Advocacy work to persuade both the general public and governments that aid is not enough to eradicate poverty is part and parcel of Christian Aid's response to the Middle East. Some of Christian Aid's partners, Israeli and Palestinian, monitor human rights abuses. Within the UK Christian Aid advocacy on the Occupied Territories and Israel has included production of a video and the building up of a network of supporters interested in the region, encouraging people to write to key decision makers, and organizing supporter visits to Israel-Palestine to experience the context and meet partners for themselves.

---

6 The General Synod will debate the Israel-Palestine issue at its meeting in November 2001.
[7] The others are the two Catholic agencies, CAFOD and SCIAF.

4.5   Living stones

Pilgrimage to the Holy Land is a large and contentious subject. Something like 300,000 visitors go from Britain in most years, and many more in the Jubilee/Millennium year 2000. About 20per cent are likely to be on pilgrimage, i.e. upwards of 60,000 in any one year. The ignoring of indigenous Christians by 95 per cent of these "pilgrims" led to the growth of the "living stones" movement to promote contact and relationship with Palestinian Christians and broaden the understanding of "pilgrimage" from the visiting of a succession of archaeological sites and Christian shrines and meditations in the footsteps of Jesus. Christian Aid and the Churches' Commission on Mission have added their resources to those of several small para-church bodies that have been promoting contact with the "living stones". The Millennium year saw many special "Pilgrim 2000" visits promoted through a number of CTBI member churches. The breakdown of the Oslo Peace Process and the violence that broke out in September 2000 has had a grievous economic impact on this movement, rendering Jerusalem's Old City, Bethlehem and Nazareth virtual ghost towns in terms of visitors.

4.6   Iraq and other Middle East concerns

A range of other subjects has figured in the agenda of the Middle East Forum of the Churches' Commission on Mission, part of the CTBI. These have included the experiences of Christian minorities such as the Copts in Egypt and the Suriani of Tur Abdin, south east Turkey. The main focus has, however, been the continuing plight of the Iraqi people, suffering at the hands of both their own government and UN-approved sanctions.

From the time of the Gulf War Christian concern for Iraq within the CTBI family has regularly surfaced – from the Quakers' early (1991) and the Church of Scotland (1992, 1995) questioning of the imposition of sanctions on a defeated nation to later Roman Catholic, Reformed and Anglican expressions which critiqued British Government policy on the inefficacy and immorality of the sanctions regime then in place. In December 1999 a letter was sent to the Prime Minister, signed by five CTBI Presidents, expressing this serious disquiet, and was followed up by the meeting with the relevant Foreign Office minister.

The humanitarian situation in Iraq has remained under close scrutiny, a process aided, inter alia, by two particular denominational initiatives. The first was the Church of England's secondment of Dr Charles Reed, its International and Development Affairs Secretary, to the United Nations Development Programme in Baghdad for six weeks in the spring of 2000. The second was the participation of Fr Frank Turner, Assistant General Secretary, Catholic Bishops' Conference of England and Wales, in a Caritas Europa delegation to Iraq in January 2001.

Chapter 4

Travel Diary

1.   Lebanon Diary, 10-14 March

Saturday, 10 March

CTBI group: Robert Davidson, Christopher Gillham, Esther Hookway, Sigrid Marten, Charles Reed, Paul Renshaw, Frank Turner, John Waller.

At 9.00pm we flew into Beirut's sparklingly redeveloped airport, were met by a representative of the Middle East Council of Churches and driven to the Near East School of Theology which was to be our home for the next five nights. NEST, American Presbyterian in origin, is located in the Hamra district, a short distance from the American University of Beirut, for which NEST serves as the Theology Faculty. Ahead of us lay three full days, beginning with a field visit to the south, the region occupied by Israel from 1982 until May 2000.

The "Liberated" South
Sunday, 11 March

The journey to Southern Lebanon enabled us to ask Suad Hajj Nassif and Elie Azouz, accompanying MECC staff, about the impact of the occupation. Around 800,000 people had been displaced and were settled either in Beirut or in the area surrounding Salda. The lack of economic investment in Southern Lebanon, alongside the collapse of the local economy following Israeli's withdrawal in May 2000 meant that most internally displaced people were unlikely to return. As Suad put it, *"returning to the south would be a displacement too far".* The transitory nature of Salda and its surrounding area was underlined when driving past Ein el Hilweh, the largest (Palestinian) refugee camp in Lebanon with 70,000 residents.

Passing through Hizbollah "charity stops" at Nabatiyet et Tahta was a reminder of the power vacuum that had been created in the south by the Israeli's withdrawal and the unwillingness of the Lebanese Government, conceivably under orders from the Syrian Government, to respond to this situation. The military excursion by Hizbollah on 7 October 2000 in the disputed Sheba'a Farms sector and the heavy bombardment by Israel and resumed excursions into Lebanese airspace were seen by our MECC friends as signs that the south is in danger of coming full circle. In the next few days we were to notice a growing debate within Lebanon about Syria's continued military presence.

MECC staff warned us about straying too far from the road when taking photographs of snow-capped Mount Hermon. Landmines cause daily human suffering and also make the land for the most part unusable. (The Israelis left no maps.) De-mining is a labour and capital intensive process, both of which are in short supply. The international community's response to this problem allegedly amounts to a dozen sniffer dogs which, if true, does not seem quite enough. Yet despite this danger, the once fertile landscape, now ravaged by Israel's security policy of deforestation, provides a home for a few pockets of olive groves which enable some resilient farmers to eke out a living.

The problems facing the south were epitomised by the village of Marjeyoun. Prior to the occupation Marjeyoun had a population of 35,000 people, 90 per cent Christian. By the time of Israel's withdrawal it was 3,500. The lack of a "national response" to Southern Lebanon threatens to push this number below 3,000. We reached Marjeyoun in time to catch the last part of the well-attended Greek Orthodox service which was also broadcast throughout the village from loudspeakers on the church tower. Following the service the CTBI delegation discussed with Bishop Kfouri and Greek Catholic Archbishop Hayek their perceptions of life after Israel's withdrawal – liberation according to Hizbollah, "liberation" according to Bishop Kfouri.

According to Bishop Kfouri "liberation" had been "like a dream", but this feeling had given way to a growing sense of disillusionment with the Lebanese Government in Beirut. Improving the condition of youth was a major problem. Most children had known nothing but occupation, while the lack of education and employment opportunities encouraged many teenagers to leave the area to study or work in the capital or abroad. Very few returned. *"The land is not for us, "* they say. *"The country is not ours. Why should we stay. "* Archbishop Hayek explained this gloom, suggesting that *"the biggest psychological problem facing Christians is their self-perception as losers. They feel losers militarily, constitutionally, economically and socially. This is what has fuelled the emigration. "* The solution, the Archbishop suggested, was for churches overseas to stand in solidarity with Christians so strengthening their resolve to stay. Day one…and Christian emigration was already on our minds.

Following lunch the delegation visited the notorious al-Khiam prison. Our escort and tour guide was Ahmed, an ex-prisoner and member of Hizbollah, who spoke in sometimes graphic detail of the harsh conditions and sub-human treatment, which guards of the Israeli-sponsored South Lebanese Army (Christian as well as Muslim), had inflicted on political prisoners. Speaking through an interpreter Ahmed told stories of great violence and sexual assault inflicted on prisoners. Even if only partially true, life in al-Khiam prison must have been unbearable. The psychological damage experienced by Ahmed, whom we took to be of Iranian rather than Lebanese origin, was revealed when he said, *"Thirty years from now there will be no Israel. They have two choices. They can leave or they can die. Since they are cowards they will leave."*

We pushed on from al-Khiam to Bamhosy, a small village on the Israeli border where we were received by a local Sunni family who gave an insight into what it had meant to live under the occupation. While "liberation" had brought political freedom the now closed border between Israel and Lebanon was creating significant economic problems for the area. We were told that there were no substantial inter faith problems in the region as *"Christians and Muslims alike suffered together because of the occupation".* We looked out from the owner's house at the red topped roofs of Israeli settlements across the border and mused on why these had been built for Russian immigrants so close to the front-line.

That evening the delegation was entertained by Dr Mary Mikhael, the Syrian-born President of NEST, who introduced the group to many of the culinary delights of the region. Lebanese hospitality knows no bounds!

Corridors of power, religious and temporal
Monday, 12 March

Beirut's geography/history came alive as we criss-crossed the city trying to avoid the traffic jams. (Beirut must be one of the few capital cities with no underground system.) Hotels and apartment blocks newly built with oil money from the Gulf as well as from Nigeria stood empty, cheek by jowl with properties damaged by shell and bullet during the civil war.

The first of our hour-long meetings was with the Grand Mufti of the Lebanese Republic for the Sunni Community, Sheikh Mohammed Rashid Kabbani. Sitting in the reception room highly decorated in abstract Islamic style, we were given a brief but comprehensive overview of Middle Eastern history as seen through the eyes of an Arab Muslim leader. The Mufti explained that, as a small country with 18 different religious groups, Lebanon is unique and has an important role to play in fostering good regional inter faith relations in the region. *"When Christian-Muslim relations are at ease in Lebanon then this has a ripple effect throughout the Middle East."*

He argued that most of the region's problems stem from the process of de-colonisation and Britain's decision to give Palestine to European Jews, rather than to Palestinians or even to Arab Jews. *"If the United Nations took a large part of Britain,"* he challenged *"and gave it to some other people, would you accept it?"*

In the Antelias district of Beirut we met HH Aram I Keshishian, Catholicos of the Armenian Apostolic (Orthodox) Church in Cilicia and the Moderator of the Central Committee of the World Council of Churches. In explaining what it means to be "Church" in the Middle East today, Catholicos Aram stressed that Christianity is an integral part of Middle East life and not a Western missionary creation. It was thus more important to talk about Christian presence rather than mission in the Middle East. Leaning forward in his chair the Catholicos mused, *"I don't understand why some Western churches have mission departments. The whole of the Church should be engaged in mission."*

Catholicos Aram went on to talk about the declining numerical strength of the Christian community, which required renewed ecumenical cooperation and a willingness to tackling contentious but relevant issues such as human rights. In Lebanon inter faith dialogue had traditionally occurred within academic circles but this dialogue now needed to be rooted in the schools and the market places so as to combat the growth of "Islamic fundamentalism", which he saw as a reaction against modernity. When pressed on the Middle East peace process and the role of the EU as a potential interlocutor, Catholicos Aram stated *"there is only one player in the Middle East and that is the USA. The EU has been marginalised, even though the Arabs want the EU to play a more active role."*

Our final meeting before lunch was with Sheikh Rafik El-Hariri, the Prime Minister of the Lebanon, who received us at his offices at the Grand Sarrayya. We had expected this meeting to be no more than a 15-minute courtesy call, but were privileged to meet with him for 50 minutes. The meeting gave us a valuable opportunity to play back many of the points that had been made to us during the previous day while also raising issues concerning the recent election in Israel. We were joined at the meeting by the Revd Dr Riad Jarjour, the General Secretary of the Middle East Council of Churches.

Mr Hariri told us of the considerable economic and financial problems facing Lebanon, not least its high national debt ($22.4bn.), to which the government was responding through privatisation and various public-private finance initiatives. Despite the premier's charisma, only time will tell whether his theory of recovery through growth will provide the answer to Lebanon's problems.

We enquired as to the role which the churches could play in easing the country's welfare problems. Betraying somewhat his financial background, the Prime Minister replied, *"well, it depends on how much money you want to spend!"* Rather than pursuing this line of inquiry we changed tack and pressed him on recent developments in the Middle East peace process.

Over the last ten years Lebanon had, Mr Hariri said, prepared its people for peace. Despite Israel's withdrawal from the south, though, regional peace continued to be elusive. Ariel Sharon's victory had been a shock. *"We want peace,"* Mr Hariri said, *"but we don't know how to handle Israel. If he's ready for peace then so are we. However, what he is doing to the Palestinians, by ring fencing their homes, is not encouraging, in fact it's sick."* Sharon's victory, he ventured, suggested that Israel had yet to take the *"quantum leap"* required for a comprehensive peace settlement. *"If you make peace in your mind then you don't mind about a few metres of land here and there."*

In response to questions on the presence of Hizbollah in the south, Mr Hariri commented that *"disarming Hizbollah would make Israel too comfortable"*. He assured us, however, that the view of Israel we had heard at al-Khiam from Ahmed was unrepresentative and that even Hizbollah had repudiated that position.

Following this meeting the delegation retired to NEST for lunch and preparation for the 90-minute Ecumenical Forum meeting in the evening. Twenty MECC staff and others locally associated with it attended. After hearing from a range of MECC staff talk about different facets of their work, the meeting was dissolved into small informal group discussions which continued during the buffet which followed, a welcome change from the formal meetings of the morning and an opportunity to test initial impressions.

Prelates and Refugees
Tuesday, 13 March

A day of competing and contrasting experiences. Traffic jams and urban geography meant that we were continually playing "catch up" with the itinerary.

The day started with a 10.00am meeting with Bishop Elias Audi, the Greek Orthodox Bishop of Beirut. Bishop Audi explained that during the Lebanese civil war the Church played an important role bridging the communal divide. As a bishop living in Tripoli at the time he had become *"very well acquainted with death"*. The role of the Church he thought was *"to live exclusively with its people regardless of the situation and regardless of the danger, even if this brought martyrdom".* Playing down the significance of the religious dimension to the civil war, the bishop expressed criticism of the West for fuelling the conflict by supplying arms.

Although Bishop Audi thought it was too soon to talk about the legacy of the war it was clear that Christian emigration to Europe had emerged as a major problem, the Christian community having fallen from 50 per cent to about 27 per cent of the total population. The Christians feel alienated from the country and, rightly or wrongly, that the electoral system is rigged against them. Those who move to Europe to study sometimes return to Lebanon while those who move to Australia, the United States and Canada are normally *"lost to Lebanon forever".* The constitutional power-sharing arrangements between Christians and Muslims were seen, he felt, as increasingly hard to justify. Accordingly, he repeatedly told his congregation that *"you have to be nationalists. If you are not nationalist in a positive way, you do not love your country".*

We then made our way to Kaslik University in Jounieh, north of Beirut, to meet with the Foundation for Human and Humanitarian Rights. Central to FHHR's advocacy and educational work is the premise that only through building a stronger civil society can Lebanon exert its political independence vis-à-vis Syria. It was therefore encouraging to hear that all students at Kaslik University are obliged to take a course on human rights. This seemed particularly important given the allegations of some that respect for human rights in Lebanon is regressing rather than improving.

Traffic considerations regrettably forced the curtailment of the encounter with FHHR in order to make a lunch appointment with Bishop Boulos Matar, the Maronite Bishop of Beirut and Greek Catholic Archbishop Kyrillos Salim Bustros of Baalbek. The meeting gave the delegation the opportunity to press the bishops on the public intervention of the Maronite Patriarch, Cardinal Nasrullah Boutros Sfeir, in September 2000 concerning the situation of Christians in the country, the high levels of Christian emigration and the continuing Syrian presence. Bishop Matar responded to a question regarding the size of the Christian community in Lebanon by saying that *"we deal with figures in a 'political' way, but we accept that we are not the majority".*

Bishop Matar suggested that many of Lebanon's problems are political. *"Lebanon is an orbit country of Syria. No decision is taken in Lebanon without prior approval from Damascus. You cannot become a Member of Parliament in Lebanon unless Syria does not approve you first. Since Syria doesn't have a democracy how can you expect to have a democracy in Lebanon."*

Following lunch the delegation was escorted round the Palestinian refugee camps of Sabra-Shatila by Mrs Sylvia Haddad, Director of the Joint Christian Committee for Social Work in Lebanon. She explained how MECC and the Lebanese churches have responded to the presence of the Palestinian refugees. It was clear, however, that despite ecumenical and other NGO efforts to fill gaps in the markets by providing kindergarten facilities, computing classes and hairdressing and other courses, the level of economic disenfranchisement of the Palestinian community meant that life inside the camps was precarious and fraught with difficulties. Palestinian refugees are denied access to 72 professions within Lebanon.

The fragility and desolation of camp life was embodied by Mohammed, a Palestinian refugee who lost both parents in the 1982 massacre. At 22 years old Mohammed's hair is already greying. His hatred towards Lebanon for keeping him in a state of political and economic impoverishment rivals his hatred of Israel. *"I'd rather live in Palestine under an Israeli flag than here under a Lebanese flag. If I had to kill someone to leave this camp then I wouldn't hesitate to do so. For me Lebanon is the worst country in the world."* Further insights into camp life were provided by our meeting with Abu Hani, the Head of the Popular Committee, which was responsible for overseeing the running of the camp.

That evening the delegation met with members of the Christian-Muslim Dialogue Committee. The CMDC was formed in 1996 with a view to tackling religious issues with a national dimension, which might threaten the constitutionally enshrined formula of co-existence. The discussion helped to refine our understanding of communal/sectarian issues within Lebanese society. However, it left many of us wondering whether we had really grasped the reality of inter faith relations in Lebanon. Committee members (Muslim, Christian, Druze) claimed that Lebanon is living this dialogue on a daily basis. We asked ourselves whether its purpose was as much about maintaining rather than negotiating the boundaries between the religions. Over dinner with CMDC members we were able to have more private conversations which resulted in some disclosures that inter faith matters at an inter personal level (e.g. mixed marriages) remain much more problematic than the constitutional ones.

Parting of the ways
Wednesday, 14 March

Robert Davidson, Christopher Gillham, Esther Hookway and Frank Turner left by road for Damascus; Paul Renshaw by air for Cairo.

Sigrid Marten, Charles Reed and John Waller remained in Beirut for an extra day. MECC organized a visit to some development project work up on Mount Lebanon.

This excursion gave a clearer insight as to the work of the MECC and the difficult environment within which it works. It also brought us into contact with local Christians who gave moving testimonies as to what it means to be a Lebanese Christian. During the civil war the Christians had been driven from their homes by the Druze who then systematically destroyed the buildings. The Lebanese Government is attempting to encourage Christians to return to the villages by providing reconstruction packages. The MECC is assisting this process by giving grants to such families to pay for doors, windows, equipment and refurbishment. The hospitality and grace with which the three of us were received and the openness with which individuals shared their life stories left us feeling humbled.

Three meetings in particular made a strong impression. The first was with Dr Manoosh whose dispensary was attached to a church in the foothills of Mount Lebanon. He explained that patients paid $1-2 to the surgery as a consultancy fee while the church provided free medicine to those who could not afford it. As Dr Manoosh said, *"this church is a healing church"*.

The second meeting was with "Tony the Baker" who had received a micro-grant from the MECC to convert a bombed-out building into a bakery. We were pleased to see that business was too busy for him to take time out to meet with us, but we can certainly recommend his pizzas!

The third was with a local carpenter who had been given a micro-loan to buy equipment. Sitting in his workshop he explained that, although business was good, there were no real opportunities and, as a father, he wanted a better life for his son. He invited us back to his home where his family, despite our protestations, pressed us into having a light lunch. We concluded the meal with a hymn and a shared prayer. Returning to NEST we were dismayed to learn that the MECC is ending its micro-credit programme around Mount Lebanon because of a shortage of funds. As our MECC guide commented, *"There are just not enough starving children in*

Mount Lebanon for donors to think that the programme is worthwhile. It's just not sexy enough."

The journey back to NEST was tortuously slow because of the numerous roadblocks that we had to go through on account of the student demonstrations being held that day. These demonstrations provided the context to our final afternoon and evening in Beirut.

Back at NEST we had a further meeting with Dr Wael Kheir, the founder of the FHHR, who expanded on a number of issues he had hinted at in our previous meeting. He explained that, if one compared and contrasted past and present UN human rights reports on Lebanon, then a deterioration in human rights was noticeable. He suggested that *"within a secular state the checks and balances are provided by the State but in Lebanon these are guaranteed by the country's confessional basis. If you abolish confessionalism in Lebanon you abolish civil society, which in turn undermines democracy."* It was in this context that he expressed his concern at the declining Christian presence in Lebanon. His solution was for Lebanon to move to a federation.

We then joined Dr Kheir at a human rights meeting at the local university where representatives from various student bodies as well as human rights organizations were meeting to review the day's demonstrations. Present were journalists, lawyers, professors, teachers and students. It was interesting to see how Dr Kheir encouraged everyone to grapple with the issues at hand and to arrive at a fair and credible conclusion as to whether the authorities had overstepped the mark in their policing of the demonstrations. We were also struck by the high number of mobile phones and the use of email, which allowed the organizers to send their reports unhindered to their overseas contacts.

Thursday, 15 March

We travelled by plane to Amman, Jordan and spent the remainder of the day resting in the Grand Palace Hotel, waiting for the rest of the CTBI delegation to arrive.

2. Syria Diary, 14-16 March

Wednesday, 14 March

Robert Davidson, Christopher Gillham, Esther Hookway and Frank Turner drove to Damascus from Beirut, calling on the way at the Lebanese residence, in the hills overlooking Beirut, of HB Patriarch Raphael I Bidawid, the Chaldean Patriarch of Babylon.

Damascus occupies a plain beneath a range of hills, the limits of the city creeping up their lower slopes. Approaching from Beirut, five unrelieved miles of depressing apartment blocks sprawl gives way suddenly to the tightly-packed, picturesque streets of the old city, where no structure exceeds about three storeys, and where markets and shops rub shoulders with ancient churches and monuments, such as the crypt that marks the house of Ananias (just off "the street called Straight") – all these buildings clustering round the great compound of the Umayyid Mosque. Damascus claims to be the oldest continuously inhabited city on earth. Its ancient centre is bustling yet somehow placid, a welcome change from the frantic, polluted Beirut. The absence of McDonalds and Starbucks enhances the city's charm but also tells of Syria's recent isolation from the flows of world trade.

Tourism could well take off here: but few tourists could have been accommodated as happily and hospitably as we were in the peaceful Greek Orthodox Patriarchate, just outside the walls of the old city. The Patriarchate's location casts an interesting light on one major theme of our visit, the Christian-Muslim relationship, for the site was given to the church in compensation for the take-over of a Christian basilica by what became the Umayyid Mosque. In fact the mosque still contains, somewhat anonymously, the tomb of John the Baptist.

Our visit was arranged by Samer Laham, Associate General Secretary of MECC. Mrs Mahat Khoury, his predecessor, who seemed to know everyone in Damascus, was equally generous with her time. Among those we met were the British Ambassador, Mr Henry Hogger and his wife, with his Chaplain, the Revd Stephen Griffith, Patriarch Ignatius IV Hazim of the Greek Orthodox Church, Bishop Batikha of the Greek Catholic (Melkite) Church, the Revd Peter Zaour, an Evangelical pastor, and Grand Mufti Khuftaro of the Abu Nour Mosque.

The Syrian Political Climate
Syria occupies the northern part of the former Ottoman province of the same name. President Hafez al-Assad's rule (1970-2000) was commonly labelled "repressive but stable". We heard that Syria is now seeking economic modernization, but without any concomitant loosening of the regime's political control. Political dissidence can still attract nasty consequences but we were told that the prevailing casualness, including that of the regime itself, is such that people are no longer cowed. Political jokes have begun to be heard in the streets as people lose their fear of the ubiquitous informers. As someone said, *"We are still under martial law, but*

it doesn't feel like that". This gradual opening-up of the public sphere has been encouraged by the new President Bashar al-Assad, though the regime's dilemma is how to relax its repressiveness without quite admitting to that process. Nevertheless President Bashar began his leadership by declaring an amnesty for some seven hundred political detainees.

Syria is still dominated by the military. Dr Adnan Umran, the Minister of Information, told us that the military takes 50 per cent of Syria's public expenditure (others put the figure higher). *"This was,"* he said, *"like living on one kidney".* Many Russian military advisers remain in Syria (for example maintaining old Soviet equipment) though Syrian links with the former USSR transcend the military sphere. Many Syrians graduated from Russian universities and many Syrian bureaucrats were trained in Moscow.

Palestinian Refugees, Lebanon, Israel

In each Arab country we visited, our party kept in mind the crisis in the Israeli-Palestinian Peace Process. One key element of that crisis is the plight of Palestinian refugees. We had seen, in Beirut, how grim their life could be. We were surprised to learn that more Palestinian refugees live in Syria than in Lebanon, but they are much better integrated and are not, for example, systematically excluded from the labour-market. Officially, any Arab is welcome to live in Syria – and this promise is largely borne out – though we understood that Syria would not welcome any new influx of Palestinians. But virtually no Palestinians would return to their own land, even if peace and stability were achieved there.

In Beirut it had seemed that Syria's relationship with Lebanon was a topic on every politically-conscious tongue. For us it had been vividly summed up in a joke: *"The Palestinian says, 'Yasser Arafat is my father, Palestine is my mother and my one great hope is the liberation of Palestine'. The Syrian says, 'President Assad is my father, Syria is my mother and my one great hope is the liberation of the Golan'. But the Lebanese says, 'President Assad is my father, Syria is my mother and my one great hope is to be an orphan!'"*

Naturally the subject was downplayed in Syria itself. When asked, people tended to speak of a "partnership" which could be terminated should Lebanon ever choose to do so. Yet Syria has vital interests in Lebanon, given its status as a regional power and its nervousness about Israeli regional ambitions. One government official even claimed to us that Syria intervened in Lebanon simply to protect the Christian population against the threat of a crushing attack by the Druze. It is also intolerable to Syria that Israel retains control of the Golan Heights. This is a wound which will not heal without Israeli withdrawal.

Christian Communities in Syria, and their inter-relationship

Many Syrians believe that European Christians are oblivious of the Christian presence in Syria. But Syria had a Christian majority till the twelfth century. The dominant churches were the Greek and Syrian Orthodox Churches (and all churches but the Orthodox are still regarded as "young" or even "foreign"). Catholic missionaries arrived in the sixteenth century and Protestants in the nineteenth. Under the French mandate the preferential treatment accorded to Catholicism caused tensions. It was suggested to us that many Catholics instinctively saw Christianity as somehow "European" rather than indigenous. This tendency became more significant in the years of Christian hardship in Syria, since many Catholics (often well-educated) readily considered emigrating. Now, emigration has since much diminished, not necessarily because things are better in Syria than previously, but because many Syrians have realized that they may be no better off elsewhere!

The church has far more freedom than in a country such as Egypt. As we were told, you do not get into trouble in Syria for being a Christian, only for being an opponent of the regime. The Greek Orthodox Patriarchate was rebuilt in 1993, many new churches have been built in villages, church leaders are appointed without government interference and are free to speak out as they see fit. On the other hand, whereas in Lebanon schools enjoy autonomy, in Syria the curriculum remains subject to governmental control. Christian Religious Education materials are available, but virtually no training for Christian teachers. *"It is very clear that we are in a Muslim country."*

Evangelical communities are small in Syria. Only one church, the Presbyterian, is a member of MECC and, in fact, it formally represents the other Evangelical churches to the Syrian civil authorities. Some of these churches are explicitly anti-ecumenical. In general, though, inter-church relationships were very positive and amicable. All the churches were conscious of an historical mission in Syria, to witness that the Middle East cannot be itself without Islam, nor without Christianity – indeed, as Patriarch Hazim said to us, *"not without Judaism too - though not Zionism".*

There is a flourishing culture of church-related youth groups. In the course of an Ecumenical Forum we were urged to arrange some form of youth exchanges as local Christians felt it was important to find ways of bringing young Syrian Christians into contact with their peers elsewhere.

Christian-Muslim Relationships

At the time of our visit, preparations were under way for a papal visit to Damascus in May, and discussions of this visit illustrated some of the pressures on Christian-Muslim relationships. Plans for Pope John Paul II to pay his respects at the tomb of John the Baptist in the Umayyid Mosque had been provocatively represented as his "praying with Muslims", the gesture of a Christian kneeling in the mosque being read as a claim to possession. (A US-based Arab newspaper had even made the implausible but inflammatory suggestion that the Pope would "say Mass" in the mosque!)

Some Muslims, at least, look on Christians as not fully Arab. That Europe is in turn seen in Syria as a "Christian continent" lends an unfortunate religious colouring to many political tensions. Patriarch Hazim put the point crisply: *"The Muslim world? Yes. The Christian world? Tell me where it is!"* Inter faith relationships are harmonious at the personal level: but it was inevitable, he thought, that a "religion of the book" could not accommodate easily to a faith in which even the Sacred Book is seen as somehow penultimate to the action of the Holy Spirit. Worse, many Muslims still think of Christianity as the "religion of the Crusades". In this context, said Patriarch Hazim, Christians need to set their hearts less on a dialogue about religious convictions than on a process of mutual presence: *"Look at me, not just at my beliefs".*

The inter faith highlight of our visit was undoubtedly the sequence of encounters we had with Grand Mufti Khuftaro, of the Abu Nour Mosque. He is in his late eighties, physically frail but mentally acute and spiritually impressive. We visited his residence and heard him discourse with grace and humour on the nature of true religion (a matter both of the love of God and neighbour, and of the transcendent fulfilment of human reason and knowledge). *"One hour of reflection is better than sixty years of worship, so give your powers of reflection their true scope."* In this realm of the spirit, the prophets (Abraham, Moses, Jesus, Mohammed) recognize one another as true brothers, whereas it is the clergy who have erected incompatible religions by donning "the mask of a pig" and expecting people to recognize that mask as the beauty of religious truth itself. *"You are teachers of hearts. You and I are in the same line."* His judgement on the necessity of the search for peace was uncompromising: *"Man is brother to man, whether he knows it or not."*

Some of these same themes were replayed next day where we were honoured guests at the Friday prayer in the Abu Nour Mosque. On this occasion, Robert Davidson had the burden and the honour of giving a public address in response.

He stressed what Christianity and Islam have in common, while noting that genuine and creative dialogue also require the free acknowledgement of differences. The world, and in particular the Middle East, cries out for Muslims, Christians and Jews to defend that spiritual integrity which will struggle for the peace with justice for which so many yearn but are denied.

We drove straight from the mosque to Amman, leaving Syria by a shabby border-post soon to be superseded by a glossier version. As we awaited the return of our papers in this amiably sleepy environment it was hard to understand stereotypes of Syria as a hotbed of Arab fanaticism.

3.　Egypt Diary, 10-15 March

CTBI delegation: Frederick George, Gillian Kingston, Michael Langrish, Hywel Wyn Richards (Paul Renshaw - 14-15 March only).

Saturday 10 March

Arriving at the same time as two planeloads of pilgrims returning from Mecca, we were met by one of All Saints Episcopal Cathedral's clergy who delivered us safely - if somewhat shaken by the sheer volume, speed and noise of Cairo traffic - to the cathedral guest house at 1.00 am. Four hours later came the muezzin's call.

Sunday 11 March

The 10.30am Eucharist in the cathedral was traditional Anglican in style and attended mainly by Sudanese refugees. Fred George and Gillian Kingston read the lessons. Over lunch the newly appointed bishop, the Rt Revd Mouneer Anis, once a doctor by profession who had led a hospital-based church for 15 years, explained how keen he is to develop new strategies for mission in his huge diocese and in particular to relate the worship of the church more to the culture of the people.

The afternoon saw us on our way south to Beni Suef, a city of some half a million inhabitants two hours by train from Cairo, there to be met by Sister Agapie Asaad of the Daughters of Mary. An energetic, compassionate and thoroughly pragmatic person, she has been involved with the Order since its establishment thirty years ago. Its house in Beni Suef is the base for community outreach and ministry. Here she acquainted us with the story of her work and her continuing struggle to secure sufficient funds to complete some ambitious projects.

Through her eyes, what appeared to be an enclosed building site was transformed into a home and school for disabled children. Some 200m. down a dusty road a two-storey building was emerging from the wooden scaffolding. In the twilight, on the second floor, we were enabled to visualize a completed old people's home down to the detail of the garden that would be planted in the central courtyard. Sister Agapie explained "*It's only two storeys so far but you can never tell how much need there will be in the future so I've ensured that the foundations will hold five storeys. If you get the foundations right then you need not worry about the future.*" We asked about the financing of such ambitious projects; the answer inspired us to quote, one at the same time, from Matthew 10:16.

We spent the night at the Bayad Coptic Orthodox Church retreat and conference centre. Based in the centuries old St Mary's Monastery built on the banks of the Nile, the centre is used by the Coptic Orthodox Diocese to provide conference, training, meeting and retreat facilities for individuals and groups.

The Centre's Director, Fr Youssef, and two other priests, joined us for a meal, together with two nuns. One of the nuns was a trained doctor who, we were told, had failed to find work because she is a Christian, even though there is a chronic shortage of doctors. The situation of the Christian minority in Egypt has been difficult for many years. There are always elements within the Muslim majority who regard Christians as belonging to an alien faith and culture. As a result Christians seem to make an extra effort to prove that they are good Egyptians, take great pride in their history and especially in the fact that the church is among the oldest living establishments in Egypt.

The missionary work of the church is clearly hampered by legislation that bans evangelizing, mixed marriages, conversion from Islam to Christianity, and takes away pension and inheritance rights from Christian widows of Muslim men who cling to their faith. These were grievances mentioned many times. In spite of this the Coptic Church is active in social work within Christian and Muslim communities, not as a means of proselytizing but "*because the need is there*". The present difficulties of obstructive officials and tiresome bureaucracy were viewed in the context of 2000 years of history and accepted as "*a cross to bear joyfully*", a phrase that was echoed time and again. It was also one of the first times when the matter of "double standards" of the West's dealing with Israel and Iraq was raised - in a gentle, but pointed way.

Monday 12 March

The following morning we travelled to Beni Suleiman, a village on the outskirts of Beni Suef - and were escorted by four soldiers. (The government is very keen to prevent any further attacks on "tourists" or Westerners). Members of the community have formed themselves into an action committee to improve the life and the standards of the village. They are helped by the Coptic Evangelical Organization for Social Services (CEOSS) the largest and possibly the most influential development NGO in Egypt which was started 50 years ago by the Protestant churches, but is now an independent organization and a long-time partner of Christian Aid.

Project work ranges from providing running water and toilets to literacy classes, the evidence of which was seen on the walls of a nearby house where the children had written *"Plant a tree and help it grow"* and *"Use the toilet not the street"*.

The main project under construction was a garden centre to provide villagers and farmers with plants to grow for food and trees to improve the environment. They were an enthusiastic group and, in a predominantly Muslim village, the women were very active and influential. It was one of them who replied to a query about Christian-Muslim relations with the comment *"It's not our religion that matters here, but our common humanity".*

Why?

Our welcome at the village of Beni Suleiman left nothing to be desired. They were clearly delighted to see us, and proudly ushered us to their new community centre, so new that our chairs sank into the freshly laid concrete!

Through the CEOSS official who accompanied us and translated, we were able to discuss issues of development and self-help, we talked about the environment and the value of planting trees, we listened to details of education and health programmes. Then there came a moment or two for a more general exchange, the nature of our visit, where we would be going next, perceptions of what was happening in the Middle East in general. Both women and men joined in lively conversation.

And it was here, in a small village in Middle Egypt, that we were asked for the first of many, many times why the West exercises a double standard with regard to the countries of the Middle East. If the West can apply sanctions to Iraq for invading Kuwait, why not to Israel for her treatment of the Palestinians? Why does Israel go unchecked ? Why?   *GMK*

At the nearby village of Azhary, literacy, health promotion and nutrition programmes are supported by the Coptic (Orthodox) Organization for Services and Training (COST). We were intrigued by a group of men who pressed us to follow them along a narrow path past two fields and across a stream to where, under the shelter of some trees, were two dozen bee hives. COST had provided them with two swarms and a basic course in bee-keeping. Now the two dozen hives provided welcome income for three families. We were reminded of what CEOSS and COST officials had told us repeatedly, that development is getting people to do things for themselves. In another home the family had been provided with a sewing machine. Admittedly it did not look used at the time of our visit. And Sister Agapie was rather put out at the state of the house: *"It is a Christian home and they should set an example of cleanliness and dignity!"*

To the end Sister Agapie never ceased to surprise us. Seeing what was obviously a place for worship we asked how long it had taken them to get permission to build a sanctuary. *"Sanctuary, what sanctuary? This is where we play table tennis. Of course there are times when we need spiritual guidance to play in the right spirit."* Indeed "innocent as doves ....."

Being escorted to the station by a nun and a soldier was a new experience. We could not fail to remark that the nun with her sewing machine, clean water, latrines, bee hives, disabled children and old peoples' homes knows more about the things pertaining to peace and a better future for Egypt.

Our return to Cairo was marked by the novel experience of being trapped in the cathedral guest house lift! We were eventually released. There are millions in Egypt entrapped in poverty.

Tuesday 12 March

None more so than the people of Hod El Henna, one of the seven rubbish-collection areas in Cairo. We were taken there by Salwa Marcos of the Bishopric of Public, Ecumenical and Social Services (BLESS), the Coptic Orthodox development organization. Words cannot convey the horror of the place. An area, perhaps three times the size of the Millennium Stadium in Cardiff, which looks like an opencast mine but is, in fact, black with decomposed garbage. It is criss-crossed by muddy roads and paths that are lined by bays where individuals and groups of all ages and sexes sort the bags of rubbish brought in by vans and donkey carts. The whole area is encircled by brick boxes with next to no amenities that are homes to 450 families - some 2,500 individuals - who literally live on and off the rubbish. Every single bag is sifted through for any thing that can be recycled.

Scraps of food and orange peel and the like are saved to feed the pigs, goats, chicken and ducks than roam through the filth and live with the indescribable stench.

In the middle of it all there is a simple church and opposite it a building that houses the priests' offices and is the base for the BLESS representatives who work with the community. It is hard to imagine anywhere where the work is more needed. The team of four young women spend their time through a variety of programmes encouraging people, who live in the most abject conditions, to believe in themselves and in the possibility of a different future for themselves and their children. We were deeply moved by their simple faith, gracious nature and their determination that things would change. They seemed surprised when asked what prompted them even to consider working in such a place, let alone keep on day after day in such horrific conditions. Pressed to answer one replied on their behalf *"The need is great and the response of the people has been very rewarding".* Hod El Henna. We could not but think of "Gehenna", and at the same time give thanks for four young women who "... *had done a fine and beautiful thing".*

Salwa sensed that we could not cope with more and so we drove to the outskirts of Cairo and the pyramids at Giza, which we were able to see against a bright blue sky. Rain the previous day, very unanticipated, had cleared away Cairo's notorious pollution for a while. It was a journey from one extreme to the other! When, the following morning we visited the Tutankhamun exhibition at the Egypt Museum, we could not but reflect on the wealth of material riches and craftsmanship that once characterized Egypt and its present-day economic and social challenges.

Pope Shenouda

Our audience with HH Pope Shenouda III, head of the Coptic Orthodox Church, reminded us of the wealth of the Christian tradition and testimony. He spoke with some force of the way Christians are treated and discriminated against in the political, economic and social life of Egypt. Yet it was clear that the Coptic Church has grown in recent years, especially through Sunday school and youth work. Pope Shenouda has appointed bishops with specific ministries in these and other fields, and we had seen for ourselves the social outreach through COST and BLESS. We also witnessed Pope Shenouda's own ability to reach out to people in his weekly "lecture" at St Mark's Cathedral where at least 5,000 attended on a Wednesday evening for a question-and-answer session followed by a scripture meditation. He is a charismatic figure who commands great respect, admiration and love from his people and is recognized by the political authorities as the official voice of the church in Egypt.

Other Christian voices
Wednesday 14 March

The Egyptian Government's virtual "sole recognition" of Pope Shenouda has its parallels in church-state relations in many other countries. In Egypt it is not wholly acceptable to the Protestant Churches as we discovered in our meeting with their President, the Revd Dr Safwat El-Baiadi. Dr Safwat made it clear that on a personal level there is a good relationship between the leaders of Protestant, Coptic Orthodox and Catholic traditions but, at grassroots level, much depended on the attitude of the local clergy. *"Denominational prejudice causes problems everywhere!"*

Within the Protestant community there is a good working relationship. School teachers meet every month to discuss their work, as do doctors to ensure that remote areas are covered. Sunday school teachers and youth workers meet regularly, there are support groups for women and prayer groups and 24-hour vigils are arranged together. Dr Safwat would welcome more cooperation, especially in the field of theological education.

The Presbyterians - the largest Protestant denomination by far - have a boys' home and 55 schools which are open to all children. Some have as many as 80 per cent Muslim students. At one time Christianity could be taught to Muslims and Islam introduced to Christians but no longer, and each school has to register a student's religion and provide a suitable teacher. Education is not free and there was some unease in response to questioning as to how children from poor homes were given the opportunity of a good education - though it was said that some effort is made in this respect.

An effort had certainly been made to try and bridge the gap between the two religious communities by arranging a summer camp for young people from Christian and Muslim backgrounds. The purpose was to try and create a less formal atmosphere for them to get to know one another by eating, playing and discussing all kinds of matters together and it was hoped to build upon the success of the first camps.

For Bishop Youhanna Kolta, Deputy Patriarch of the Coptic Catholic Church, the main issues in Egypt are economic, not religious. He believes Islamic fundamentalism has not been and will not be successful, and that this augurs well for Christianity in Muslim countries. Muslims see the "Christian" world advancing technologically and in other ways, while the Islamic world fails to do so.

Egyptians, he felt, must say yes or no to new technology, to personal freedom and equality between men and women.

Commenting on cross-cultural perceptions, Bishop Kolta averred that Muslims think that Europe is no longer Christian and that Islam will supplant Christianity. Muslims have more freedom in Europe than they do in their own countries and certainly more than they allow Christians in their own countries. London is perceived by some as being a centre for fundamental extremists, a place where people are given liberty to be fundamentalists. The British press is seen as being, on the whole, negative towards Islam abroad, but ambivalent towards it at home.

As regards peace in the Middle East, Bishop Kolta said, *"it depends on mind set: Israel needs to change its Zionist mentality".*

Thursday 15 March

The day began with a field visit to Kom Ghorab, a poor area in Cairo where CEOSS has been engaged for several years in an environmental programme among a community of potters. Their traditional furnaces were posing hazards to health. Through a process of community mobilization CEOSS have encouraged the use of more modern furnaces and the promotion of other income-generating projects. It was a good example of a Christian agency working with urban Muslims.

CEOSS is obviously one of the most important and influential NGOs in Egypt - a point underlined by its impressive headquarters in the Heliopolis district of Cairo which appeared, indeed, to be something of a public statement about CEOSS itself and its work. Obviously the work is desperately needed if the mass of people are to reap the benefits of any future investment from the EU - which Egyptians expect will play an increasingly important role in the development of the economy. In discussion with senior staff it became clear that they felt the role and influence of Britain and even the USA was diminishing. Concern was voiced about the post-Mubarak period and the point was forcefully made that the days of "benevolent dictatorship" are over, that *"economic development and democratic development must go hand in had if there is to be real progress".*

The Director of CEOSS, Nabil Abadir, echoed Dr Safwat in not appearing as pessimistic as Pope Shenouda as to the position of Christians in the public life of Egypt. Indeed while they agreed that there was a perception of prejudice there is no "official" persecution and the situation is much improved to what it was 20 years ago. Three Christians have been elected to the parliament and some have been appointed to posts in the university. The relationship between Egypt and other

Arab countries has certainly improved since the days of Sadat's peace treaty with Israel. But keeping the balance in the relationship between Egypt as an Arab-Muslim country on the one hand and with the powers that will help Egypt grow as a country able to compete economically with Israel on the other is a very difficult matter.

Nabil Abadir seemed certain that Israel would eventually sign a peace treaty with the Palestinians, a move which will change the whole Middle East scene. Dr Safwat felt that Israel had trapped itself by failing to understand the Arab/Islamic mind and the importance of the Al-Aqsa Mosque. Neither did it understand that *"Negotiation means that you don't get all you want. The West should realize that pictures of children throwing stones and being killed by guns and tanks are very powerful and provoke powerful response in Egypt. Before condemning the stone throwers it should be remembered that when young people lose hope they also lose respect for life."*

Again the difference in attitude of the British Government towards Iraq and Israel was questioned, and the apparent forgetfulness of the churches of the Palestinians' plight. When it was pointed out that the churches had made statements about the situation it was clear that they were unaware of them. It was impressed on us that statements should be sent directly to the churches in Egypt so that they can defend themselves against attacks in the press, e.g. that the churches invariably support Israel. The perception certainly persists within the Christian and Muslim community in Egypt that the British and Irish churches are more ready to support Israel than Palestinian Christians.

One of our last visits was to the Old Coptic Churches of Cairo, several of which are being renovated with government financial support in a bid to boost the tourist industry. The "living stones" of the indigenous churches are still having a difficult time with restrictions of all kinds on church building, improvement and renovation, though some signs of easing can be recognized.

We had an opportunity before flying to Jordan to convey our sincere thanks to the staff of the Middle East Council of Churches who had chaperoned us during our stay and transported us safely from one destination to another through the terrifying Cairo traffic. Our spiritual journey had at times been even more harrowing but was, in all respects, enriching and truly rewarding.

4.   Jordan Diary, 15 –17 March

We arrived in Jordan late on Thursday evening, 15 March, for a 36-hour stay en route to Palestine-Israel. Compared to Cairo we found Amman clean, spacious and prosperous, and the mood of the city appeared to be more relaxed and secure. The teams of workers cleaning the streets and painting the kerbstones were impressive, but that was all for the benefit of the Arab summit the following week and not for CTBI!

Jordan has borders with Iraq, Israel, Saudi Arabia, Syria and the West Bank. The Hashemite Kingdom was created in 1946 on both sides of the River Jordan and ruled by King Hussein from 1953 to 1999. In 1948 Palestinians flooded across the river, seeking refuge in response to the first Israeli-Arab war. Nineteen years later the "Six-Day War" brought an end to Jordan's control of East Jerusalem and the West Bank and another influx of Palestinian refugees was received. Today Jordan is, with Egypt, one of the two Arab countries which have signed a formal peace treaty with Israel. It does not go unrewarded with American economic and other assistance. During our short stay we were able only to catch a glimpse of the work of the churches, especially with refugees, and speak with some of the leaders of the churches in membership with MECC.

Friday, 16 March

MECC staff, Nahla Kharmash Audeh and Edmond Adam, gave us an initial overview of the structure and work of MECC in Jordan and Iraq. Then followed a session on the same premises with Mr George Hazou and members of the Near East Council of Churches Committee for Refugee Work (subsumed into MECC's Department of Services to Palestinian Refugees but retaining its former name). Following this we went on to meet the Greek Orthodox Bishop Benedictus, and sat in on the tail end of his lecture to Sunday school teachers, before an hour with him. Our next, shorter, meeting was with the Anglican Archdeacon Salim. After a quick lunch we met with a few of the local church leaders, four Orthodox priests and a Lutheran pastor. Following this, while most of the team enjoyed a visit to the Roman Amphitheatre in central Amman, Fred George met with some leaders of the Baptist Church in Jordan, which is not a member of MECC.

Palestinian refugees in Jordan

Most of the refugees who fled when the State of Israel was created 53 years ago came to Jordan, and a great many Jordanian citizens thus have Palestinian origins. It is estimated that there are some 3.5 million refugees in Jordan. The majority has integrated into Jordanian society and are citizens with the right to live and work in

Jordan. However there are some 300,000 still in 13 camps. Gaza camp has over 25,000 refugees who fled from Gaza in 1967. They are deemed to have the right to return and are therefore not entitled to citizenship or work permits in Jordan.

Ecumenical services to refugees

MECC, through its Department of Services to Palestinian Refugees (DSPR), is involved in frontline social care and development work among refugees. Active in nine of the thirteen camps, it has programmes on health, education and awareness raising, training, capacity-building and job-creation. The unemployment rate among the refugees is high at almost 30 per cent, and prospects of finding secure employment are very limited. For many very little has changed throughout the period they have been in the camps.

We visited the Talbieh Camp with a population of 9,000, where 90 per cent are unemployed. Some are from the 1948 and others from the 1967 exodus. An old man and his son who was about 25 years of age greeted us in the street. *"What is life like in this camp?,"* we asked *"It's not good, I have never had work, and there is nothing for my son, no future."* There was hopelessness written all over their faces. DSPR has a centre at this camp which runs sewing and embroidery classes and health improvement programmes for women and young people - a tiny ray of hope on an otherwise bleak horizon.

The question of the "right to return" and the future of Palestinian refugees remains one of the most intractable issues between Israel and the Palestinians. Feelings run high when this is discussed, *"We will not give up our right to return to our land. We do not want compensation - we want justice".* This is the uncompromising stance of one refugee.

Christian-Muslim relations

Relations between Christians and Muslims appear to be cordial. The constitution provides safeguards for "all forms of worship and religious rites in accordance with the customs observed in the Kingdom, unless such is inconsistent with public order and morality." However, this freedom of religion has to be set in the context of a Constitution which states that Islam is the state religion. Proselytising or encouraging conversion to the Christian faith are prohibited and considered illegal. A Muslim person who converts to Christianity is treated as a Muslim according to the law, but the reverse is not the case. Shari'a (Islamic law) requires the death penalty for conversion, but the state law does not prescribe any penalty. However, Muslims who convert to other religions often face discrimination, threats, and abuse from their families, friends and religious leaders. Christians are subject to some aspects of Shari'a, e.g. parental rights over children and inheritance.

The Christian presence in government and society

Christians in Jordan are not subjected to any significant discrimination, and are represented in government and business at the highest level. Eleven of the eighty seats in parliament are held by Christians, (cf.3/444 in Egypt) including two Cabinet posts. Christians also hold senior positions in the army, security services and other government institutions. We were told that 40 per cent of private businesses is in the hands of Christians, including many of the major banks. This is attributed to the tolerant and supportive policy of both the late King Hussein and his son King Abdullah towards Christians. The distribution of wealth among Christians is very uneven. A few families control the wealth while the majority remain poor.

Christians make up only about three per cent of the population, while over 90 per cent are Sunni Muslim. Only the three main monotheistic religions - Islam, Christianity and Judaism - are recognized by the State. Official government recognition is granted only to the Greek Orthodox, Roman Catholic, Greek Catholic, Armenian Orthodox, Maronite Catholic, Assyrian, Anglican, Lutheran, Seventh-Day Adventist, United Pentecostal and Presbyterian Churches. Other churches (New), including Baptists, Assembly of God, Free Evangelical, Church of the Nazarene and the Christian Missionary Alliance are registered as "societies" but not as churches. Despite this they do enjoy almost the same freedoms as the recognized Churches.

Churches ancient and modern

The Ancient (Orthodox) Churches view the New Churches with deep suspicion, regarding them as just inauthentic "new invaders".

Passions ran high on discussion on the nature of the Church, its mission, evangelism and conversion. The Orthodox Churches see mission in terms of presence (the existence of the Church in the Middle East from the first century), and social action (DSPR work in the camps). There is strong opposition to those who convert from Orthodoxy to any of the New Churches because of a personal experience of faith. The latter are accused of "sheep stealing" and "fishing in our pond".

This criticism is mainly about the exodus of youth from the Orthodox Church and culture, drawn by attractive and well-resourced programmes of activities for youth in the New Churches. It was interesting to meet a Lutheran pastor and hear about his journey of faith. Born and brought up in the Greek Orthodox Church, he was educated in the Lutheran School, where he was introduced to the Lutheran Church, joined it, and is now one of its enthusiastic young pastors in Amman. There was passion and conviction in this young man. His spiritual life appeared to have been enriched by both traditions.

There is no doubt that there are in Jordan, as elsewhere in the Middle East, fundamentalist groups whose evangelistic methods are insensitive and inappropriate. Some of these also hold extreme Zionist views. But it is a great shame that all the New Churches appear to be damned by the deeds and views of some of them.

On several occasions it was alleged that members of the New Churches, were engaged in inappropriate evangelism when they distributed Christian tracts outside a mosque. This had resulted in the Jordanian security questioning the leaders of MECC about the incident. When this was raised with some Jordanian Baptists (not in MECC), they had a different version to tell. They allege that this was a deliberate act of provocation by some groups to discredit the work of Evangelical Christians. What seemed to be evident was the mistrust and hostility among the Ancient Churches towards the New Churches.

The ecumenical path is seldom free from pitfalls. The challenge of broadening ecumenical fellowship became very clear very quickly in Jordan. Meanwhile fear, myth, suspicion and jealousy have inserted themselves into inter-church relationships.

Both the Ancient and New Churches are agreed on the urgent need to encourage Jordanian Christians to remain in Jordan. The emigration of the most gifted and educated Christians, mainly men, to Europe and North America has reached crisis point in Jordan. This is one of the reasons why so many Christian women marry Muslim men. Anglican Archdeacon Salim shared his sadness at the fact that more than 1,000 Christian women marry Muslims every year.

Perceptions of the West

Once again, as in Cairo and Beni Suef, we heard the term "double standards" used to describe British government policy towards the Middle East. There is deep cynicism and mistrust of Britain, which is seen as being in the pocket of the United States. Again and again attention was drawn to British and US policy of sanctions and bombing of Iraq for ignoring UN resolutions, but taking no effective action when Turkey occupied Cyprus, Syria occupied Lebanon and Israel occupied Palestine. Oil and trade are seen to be more important than human rights and justice. Among those with whom we spoke British reputation was pretty low, despite the closeness of the official Anglo-Jordanian relationship. France, on the other hand, was appreciated for its willingness to buck the American lead over policy towards the Palestinians and Iraq.

Perceptions of the British Churches

It is generally thought that British Christians have forgotten the Christians of the Middle East. We are seen as tourists who come to see the sites, not to share fellowship and learn about the Christian community. We are perceived as being indifferent and silent on human rights and religious freedom and supporting British government policy which is seen as pro-Israel.

Some issues of perception and practice over the channelling of refugee and development assistance were vigorously raised with us. Organizations like the NECC Committee for Refugee Work in Amman wish ecumenical agencies like Christian Aid to channel such aid on principle through Middle East Church organizations. They see this as important to reinforce the witness of the Middle East churches and restore their credibility and confidence in the Middle East.

Throughout our short visit we were warmly welcomed and everyone expressed much appreciation that we were there to show solidarity and support. *"Please don't wait another twenty years before you come again,"* said Edmond Adam as he waved us goodbye at the Allenby/King Hussein Bridge.

5. Israel-Palestine Diary, 17-24 March

Jerusalem
Saturday 17 March

Our journey to the Jordan river took us via Talbieh refugee camp, St George's Church, Madaba (with its ancient mosaic floor) and Mount Nebo, with its even more ancient Mosaic view across the Jordan valley. The Dead Sea and Qumran to the left, Jericho more or less straight ahead, though it would take a zigzag route down the valley side to get to the bridge. Jericho was, however, going to be bypassed, closed as it was to outsiders for "security" reasons. Beyond stretched the dry hills of Judaea and, just out of sight, Jerusalem itself. So near yet, for our Palestine-born companions, so far.

The crossing of the border was relatively uneventful and we found the bus sent down to take us to Jerusalem. There we were accommodated at Notre Dame, the large centre of the Pontifical Institute set just outside the walls of the Old City, close to the New Gate.

At 5.00pm we were welcomed by the Rt Revd Munib Younan, the Evangelical Lutheran Bishop in Jerusalem, who chairs the International Christian Committee, part of the structures of the MECC. We also met Ramzi Zananiri, ICC Executive Secretary, our attentive minder throughout our time in Jerusalem, who had coordinated the programme.

Bishop Munib explained the reasons for the new Intifada. These he gave as disillusionment with the Oslo peace process, which promised but did not deliver peace; the sensitivities of the Camp David meeting, where Ehud Barak had adopted a different negotiating position from that he had outlined to the Knesset; and the actions of Ariel Sharon, which had been the spark which ignited the tinder of multiple Palestinian frustrations. Of the present situation the bishop said, *"We are in war – what can the international community do to help us?"* An Intifada on this scale in the USA, he added, would have brought about 35,000 deaths and 1,080,000 injuries!!

Bishop Munib went on to say that what the Palestinians wanted was the implementation by Israel of UN resolutions, a two-state solution, and the return of refugees. Help was needed with education, with inter faith dialogue. Prayer - vigil prayer - was vital. For him a key question was, *"What purpose does God have for the two per cent of the population who are Christians? Are they not called to be brokers for peace, catalysts for reconciliation, defenders of human rights, apostles of love?"*

Bishop Munib's analysis and vision were articulated with quiet emotion and conviction. We realized the depths of the situation into which we were now entering. Solidarity was not going to be comfortable.

Sunday, 18 March

This was our day off, but it was hardly a day of rest. We separated to go to morning worship in a variety of churches. Robert Davidson preached at St Andrew's (Scots Memorial Church) about the nature of truth, a subject which bore a great relevance to the many perceptions of truth which we had heard in the previous week. Afterwards a few of us looked for lunch in the Old City. It was a case of looking because many shops and eating places were not open, so small is the number of tourists and pilgrims in Jerusalem.

Some of us then went out to Yad Vashem, the national Holocaust Museum. Leaving the bright Jerusalem afternoon light and entering the dark blackness of the

The dolls......

It was the little dolls that got to me, dolls belonging to children like my daughter, loved and cuddled and taken to bed, dressed and undressed and played with, never left behind, and especially not when the owner was being taken off to a concentration camp.

The Holocaust Museum on the outskirts of Jerusalem is a harrowing place. Hundreds of photographs, personal effects, documentation, growing in horror as one moves from aisle to aisle. How, in the lifetime of many of us, could this happen in a 'civilized' continent ? How could human beings do this to other human beings?

Painful though it is, the world must remember that this has happened. There is, of course, no guarantee that it will not happen again, somewhere, by some group of people to another whom they believe not to be worth the air they breathe. There was Armenia, and there have been Cambodia, Rwanda, the former Yugoslavia.......

As we were coming out, they were going in, a group of young women, about eighteen or nineteen. They were well behaved and well dressed, any school principal would have been proud of them. But the uniform was army uniform and some of them were carrying guns. And they were going in to learn, or re-learn, as potential defenders of their nation, what another nation in another time had done to them, as the world stood by.

We looked out over the valley towards one of the many settlements which are encircling the city of Jerusalem, settlements built on illegally confiscated land, land which has often been agricultural land, farmed by Palestinians for years, if not generations.

We wondered how a people which has endured so much suffering over the centuries can now turn around and inflict such suffering on others. Does the memory of such suffering not teach something about justice and equality?

And is that memory now being used to fuel fanaticism and hatred rather than mercy and peace? Is that memory being ab-used to indoctrinate these little-more-than-children so that they see those different from themselves as threat rather than as neighbour ?

And as one nation does this to another nation in our time, is the world still standing by?

GMK

Children's Memorial and listening "among the stars" to the recitation of names of children lost in the Holocaust was dramatic and moving. When we went to the main, relentlessly sad, exhibition area we soon found our notice attracted to one inscription. Describing the situation of the Jewish people in the 1930s and 1940s, it said how terrible it was for people to be without a state, without a land and to be persecuted. How accurate a description that seemed of the plight of the Palestinians in 2001! We also witnessed a group of young Israeli women soldiers who simply wandered through, stopping from time to time to chat in a circle. It did not seem to matter to them for what hard-won cause they were now literally, at that moment, bearing arms.

Monday, 19 March -The Old City

The morning began with a walking tour of the Old City, through all four Quarters. For those who had seen it all before, even several times, it was still a different place. No crowds, few groups, most shops were empty or shut down. So much of the life had gone out of the city. But of course the buildings were there and so, ironically, it was a lot easier to see and appreciate them! [8]

At the end of the morning we went to the Haram Al-Sharif to meet officials of the Muslim Waqf, including the administrator, Mr Adnan Husseini. The Waqf oversees Muslim religious endowments, including the Dome of the Rock and the Al-Aqsa Mosque. We met, literally, in an upper room. At the foot of the stairs was a small contingent of Israeli soldiers, barring entry to the grounds of the Haram to anyone who was not Muslim. (We were told that at the time of Friday prayers Muslims under the age of 45 were not admitted either.)

These religious officials were clear about the role of Jerusalem: *"Jerusalem should be a city of peace and religious respect but these things haven't existed since 1967."* They were concerned about the severe inadequacy of municipal services given the taxes Jerusalemites had to pay, but even though the prospects for a settled future appeared remote, they asserted, *"We don't need aid - we can eat the soil to survive - what we want is dignity"*. They asked that that we, from Western churches, accept that *"It's your role to help the region from a big disaster"*.

---

8 Tourism in the year 2000 employed about 220,000 people in Israel and 10,000 in "Palestine". There was significant millennial investment in tourism in Jerusalem, Bethlehem, Jericho, Nazareth and other places. Since September 2000 the dramatic reduction in tourism to Israel-Palestine has brought severe financial crisis. Thousands of jobs have been lost. Pilgrimage companies overseas been bankrupted or forced to diversify. (Source: Alternative Tourism Group, Beit Sehour.)

After our meeting the mosque officials negotiated with the soldiers with the result that we were allowed a very short visit to the Haram - a valued glimpse but much more limited than the experience of pilgrims in the Millennium year who thronged the grounds and visited the Dome of the Rock itself.

Prospects for peace

In the afternoon we had a meeting with Drs Gershon Baskin and Zakaria Al-Qaq, two political scientists who had formed a joint think-tank (the Israel-Palestine Centre for Research and Information) during the first Intifada. Gershon said that the issues remain the same now as they were then. He explained that the weakness of the Oslo agreement was that it did not have a way of dealing with "worst-case scenarios". Both sides, in his opinion, had breached the agreement, although Israel had breached it more. The Palestinian Authority had failed to prepare its people on how the refugee issue might be solved without raising Israeli fears of being expected, in Shimon Peres' words, to "commit national suicide". At the crucial Camp David meeting Arafat and Barak had only one hour together in face-to-face meeting. Another complicating factor, he thought, was that because Arafat looked ill at around this time, a leadership struggle began among the Palestinians. People were vying for position. It may have been in this situation that Arafat needed to do deals with some of the contenders, which then tied his hands in negotiations.

Zakaria Al-Qaq began by saying, *"This conflict is important because our enemy is important"*. He indicated that the modern Palestinian problem began in 1970 and that successive efforts to resolve it had failed. Following Oslo, the fruits of peace tended to go to the leaders rather than to the people. Some "suspect" people ended up in positions of power in the Palestinian Authority. A consequence has been that people have tended to look to Hizbollah, or to Saddam Hussein, as models of leadership, rather than to Yasser Arafat. They are seen to have principles and to stick to them. He concluded with a memorable statement which we tried out on several others in the ensuing days: *"We have now moved from conflict resolution to conflict management."*

Tuesday, 20 March - Two narratives

This was a morning to engage with the political realities and we were fortunate to be able to do so at a high level. We went first to the Ministry of Foreign Affairs, where we met Mr Avi Granot, a senior policy adviser to the President of Israel. He was accompanied by a former ambassador, now in the Ministry of Religious Affairs.

Mr Granot gave the rationale for Israel's position with cool efficiency. The significance of Oslo was that it recognized that two separate nations needed to exist. That goal was to be reached by political and diplomatic means, rather than violence. However, the devil of the agreement was in the detail. He said that Ehud Barak took a great risk in proposing at the Camp David talks something which did not have the support of the Knesset or the general public. His hope was that an agreement would give him that support. It was a political gamble that had not come off . When it did not succeed, Mr Granot claimed, Yasser Arafat resorted to violence.

Israel, Mr Granot continued, is waiting for that violence to end. He claimed that Yasser Arafat controls 90 per cent of the Palestinian population" and implied that the violence is his to curtail. He accused Arafat, however, of never once calling for an end to violence and hatred. "*When did you last see him out of military uniform?*" he asked.

Mr Granot made it clear that the Government of Israel recognizes the suffering and economic difficulties of the Palestinian people in the present situation.[9] He also made clear that it is for Yasser Arafat to make the next move. There would be no Israeli compromises when shopping centres were empty because of the threat of car bombs. "*'End the violence straightaway'* may", as he put it, "*sound simple, even simplistic, but it is the only formula that works.* " He claimed that an appeal from the Jerusalem Patriarchs to Yasser Arafat to prevent violence at Christmas had resulted in 500 Palestinian police being deployed in Beit Jala – and there was no violence.

It was a quiet meeting, held in an intense atmosphere. At one point an attendant carelessly and, for a moment, locked us in a room he assumed was empty. Mr Granot got up to see what was afoot. "*We almost had a closure there!*" he said. It would have been funny but for the context.

'Closure', Mr Granot asserted, was a defence tactic, not a political tool. Indeed, any IDF firing too was always, we were told, a defensive, responsive measure and nothing more.

At many points we could have taken issue with Mr Granot, but we contented ourselves largely to asking questions for the sake of clarification, e.g.

---

9 In early April the Palestinian Finance Minister was reported as saying that the Palestinian economy had lost more than$20bn in trade and wages since September 2000, and unemployment had risen to over 50 per cent because of Israeli closures. (Source: *Jerusalem Post* 9 April 2001)

Q. *How could the Palestinians be sure that Israel would withdraw from occupied territory if an agreement was reached?*
A. Look what happened in Sinai: we withdrew once agreement with Egypt was signed. *"We will agree to the dissolution of some settlements, but we cannot yet talk about maps."* There will be no *"systematic expansion"*, though *"natural expansion as families grow"* might be necessary.

Q. *Why does Israel not obey UN resolutions?*
A. We did obey the one regarding South Lebanon. Our diplomatic conversations reveal that although countries vote for UN resolutions, many do not do so from reasons of conviction. Many indicate that really they support us. Do you realize that Israel is the only country in the world that cannot be a member of the Security Council? Despite that, Israel does respect UNSCR 242 and 338. *"In principle they are the basis."*

Q. *Why is the Israeli response to violence so strong?*
A. Do you realize what we could do? We only act in response to violence, and then at the minimum level to be effective. If there is one building standing in Beit Jala, after they fired at Jerusalem, it means we have not responded at all. You must understand that a democratic government has to offer security to its citizens.

Q. *Why is there such a disproportionate rate of death and injury among the Palestinians?*
A. We shoot better than Palestinians, that's why.

Q. *What is the Israeli Government's position on the "Right of Return"?*
A. To create a Palestinian state and to allow for the Right of Return is a nonsense. If you give millions of Palestinians the right to vote in Israel, it means that Israel ceases to exist as a Jewish State; if you deny them the right to vote you create second-class citizens, which Israel cannot accept. You cannot fight for both things at once. *"But Arafat has no boundaries."*

Mr Granot explained the Government of Israel's political position in a very professional, but also, to some of us, a rather chilling, way. The onus, from the Israeli Government's perspective, was on Yasser Arafat to "stop the violence" and thereby open the door to negotiation and the easing of restrictions on Palestinian lives. There was clearly no room for alternative perceptions. To get that we had to move on.

Our next destination was Orient House, the headquarters of the Palestine Liberation Organization in Jerusalem. It was immediately obvious how much more relaxed the security was in comparison with the Ministry of Foreign Affairs. That was surprising given that our meeting was with Dr Hanan Ashrawi, a major spokesperson for the Palestinian cause on the world stage.

In her opening talk and in answering questions Hanan Ashrawi articulated the Palestinian cause with warmth, clarity and humanity. *"When we reach rock bottom and think things cannot get any worse,"* she said, *"we discover we are wrong."* She spoke about the fact that no UN resolutions relating to the Palestinians have been implemented and about the illegality of the Jewish settlements. She argued that, in any case, their size and positioning (not least in relation to water supplies) makes it impossible to create any viable Palestinian state. Challenged with Avi Granot's example of Sinai, she pointed out that, in that case, Israel was dealing with a sovereign state (Egypt) and that part of the process of withdrawal was the destruction of the settlements in Sinai. That would hardly be feasible on the West Bank! Interestingly, in talking of settlements, she described the Israeli settlers as ideological rather than economic settlers. In Galilee exactly the opposite view was expressed.

Asked to respond to Avi Granot's clarification of official Israeli policy on the Right of Return, Dr Ashwari made three points: *"What State expects the legal right to guarantee ideological dominance? Why should the Palestinians be obliged to function as the guardians of Zionism? In any case, UNSCR 194 allows the return to people's actual homes, not merely to some separate homeland, on the condition that they are willing to live in peace."*

She rejected Israeli accusations about alleged "anti-Israeli" bias in Palestinian school books and claimed that Israeli textbooks often excluded any reference to Palestinians, maintained a false myth of the "birth of Israel" and, in some cases, viciously dehumanised Palestinians.

On two points Hanan Ashrawi was particularly powerful. She referred to the media criticism of Palestinians for allegedly using children as a shield in front of their snipers, ensuring that when Israeli soldiers returned fire it would be children who were injured or killed. *"What sort of mothers do they think we are,"* she asked, *"that we would allow our children to be used in that way? Do they think we don't love our children?"*

Dr Ashrawi spoke openly of her own position regarding the Palestinian Authority, in which she served for a limited time before resigning. Her view is that what is needed is open and transparent government, and that is not what is on offer at the moment. State security courts deliver summary justice to those alleged to be

collaborators. Sometimes the PA harasses people *"just to please the other side"*.
In her view the PA seriously lacks credibility in the Palestinian community. Her
dissent clearly was not about goals but about ethos and method.

Putting the differences in personality on one side, having listened to them both it
was hard to see how the gap between the two understandings could be bridged. It
was therefore a considerable encouragement that we heard another speaker before
we left Orient House, a young researcher working on what he described as "Track
Two" negotiations. It was good to realize that, despite the tensions brought about
by the election of Ariel Sharon in February, efforts were still going on to try to find
negotiated paths through the labyrinthine residues of history, prejudice and
competing objectives.

Two development agencies

After a quick lunch in the Old City we met with Dr Tom Neu (American Near East
Refugee Aid) representing the Association of International Development Agencies
(AIDA) and Maha Aby Dayyeh (Women's Centre for Legal Aid and Counselling),
representing Palestinian NGOs. Tom Neu told us that there are some 45
development agencies in AIDA, each with a development purpose, each with an
overseas home base and a representation in Jerusalem, and each with a registration
with the authorities on both sides. The situation in Israel/Palestine is such that
there is, for the size of population, a very high number of NGOs. Maha told us that
at the moment the focus of effort had to be on the consequences of the emergency.
The closures sometimes make the movement of relief supplies very difficult. Some
60 per cent of the people were living under the poverty line;[10] olive and eucalyptus
trees have been destroyed for "security" reasons, depriving people of livelihood;
the tourist trade has been decimated. But there is a will to survive at all levels. One
of the effects of the Intifada has been to increase community spirit.

Five church traditions

A session with several leading Jerusalem church figures enabled us to gain an early
impression of their concerns in the present situation. They represented the Greek
Orthodox, Armenian Apostolic, Syrian Orthodox, Maronite and Coptic Orthodox
Churches. The discussion took in several issues.

The first was the complexities in the Christian-Muslim relationship. On the one
hand the longevity of Christian presence and witness alongside Muslims cannot be
discounted. Today there is unity in the struggle but, after that, what? The rise of

---

10 In February the UN had said that 1:3 Palestinians live on less than $2.10 a day, compared to a 1:5 ratio six
months earlier. (Source: *Jerusalem Post* 9 April 2001)

religious fanaticism elsewhere is a concern but at present the Christian-Muslim relationship is, according to Greek Orthodox Metropolitan Timothy, *"exemplary"*.

The way in which Yasser Arafat speaks in conciliatory terms about Christians' place in the region is appreciated. But there is uncertainty about the new proposed constitution of the State of Palestine in which there is *"no space at all for Christians. We want to be rooted here not just by tradition but by law ... We don't expect to be at ease in this context at any time .... it is part of our cross, our reality, assuming this responsibility as lovingly as we can."* (Maronite Archbishop Paul Sayyah)

Archbishop Sayyah, who is practically engaged in inter faith work at the youth level, said that Christians in the Middle East have an identity problem. They *are "neither here nor there"* - and warned us against expecting a black and white picture.

As regards the Intifada, Archbishops Sewerios (Syrian Orthodox) and Sayyah agreed on the desperate state of affairs that was looming without rapid development in peace-making. *"We hope for peace soon if only to help the people catch their breath,"* said Archbishop Sewerios. He saw the need for the clergy to *"feel the weight of the people".* After all, *"If the church becomes too comfortable it would forget its spirituality!"*

Metropolitan Timothy said that the people want to see practical steps taken towards relief and suffering. He regretted the disparity in resources that led to some difficulties in relationship between the churches and admitted the need for a more common approach.

The Israeli peace lobby lives!
The election of Ariel Sharon in February 2001 was evidence of a very significant collective shift to the Right by the Israeli electorate. Many of the post-Oslo peace movement voted for Likud as well, believing that Yasser Arafat alone had been responsible for the breakdown in the Camp David talks. Yet there are Israelis who remained firm in their commitment to peace with justice for all within Israel and the Occupied Territories.

One of these is Terry Greenblatt, Director of Bat Shalom (Daughters of Peace). This is an Israeli non-profit organization which since 1994 has tried to work in close partnership with a similar Palestinian organization, the Jerusalem Centre for Women. Terry explained in our last meeting of the day that "holding the two narratives" is vital but difficult. *"You have to remember the asymmetry in the room at all times".* The two organizations, known together as 'The Jerusalem Link' had worked through the sharing of many basic principles, but had not yet managed jointly to address the Right of Return issue. As Terry put it, *"for Jewish Israelis this is the issue that propels them from the 'comfort zone' to the basic components of identity. Zionism needs to be taken down and discussed- its past, present and future - and the prices paid evaluated."* She also held up a vision of women playing a stronger role in negotiation, *"women will remain at the table longer!"*

Bat Shalom has been calling for years for international protection for Palestinians, not least so as to be able to answer the question that will come in time - *"What did we do?"* Terry expressed concern about arms sold to Israel, and the possibility that Zionism will not feature adequately in the World Conference on Racism and Xenophobia (September 2001*). "If the international community allows that to happen, it is not OK. There must be a way that Israel can be honourably helped to the same standards as other countries...its special status is not conducive to proper accountability."*

The whole day left us with much for our minds and hearts to digest, but it was time to attend to other needs. We had agreed to eat out and set off to see if we could find a restaurant open in the Old City. Most doors and shutters were shut but, in the end, we found ourselves invited by a restaurant owner onto his hitherto closed rooftop. He was glad of the custom and we were glad of the chance to relax at the end of a full, fascinating and disturbing day. We looked forward to the next two days and the different experiences they would bring - to some in Gaza, to others in Galilee and to the rest in Bethlehem, Hebron and Jerusalem.

Gaza Diary
Wednesday 21 March

CTBI group: Michael Langrish, Sigrid Marten, Hywel Wyn Richards, Frank Turner,

After a two-hour journey from Jerusalem we arrived at the Eretz crossing where even moving through the VIP channel reminded one member of the border crossing into East Germany 15 years ago.

Ibrahim Ghandour and Mr Mahmoud Okshiyya from the local NECC Committee for Refugee Work were on hand to introduce us to Gaza. We were reminded of the severe problem of overcrowding in the Gaza Strip, 365sq.km in area and is home to 1.2million people (over 800,000 of them refugees) - the world's most densely populated area.

Gaza is designated as territory of the Palestine Authority yet 42 per cent of the land is taken for 19 Jewish settlements with an overall population of 4000 (guarded by more than 6000 troops). These settlers pay no tax to the Palestinian Authority, and even their security costs are paid by the PA. There is water for their swimming pools while many Palestinians are without adequate supplies for drinking and sanitation. Roads and land are still being taken over for the protection and use of the settlers. GDP in Gaza has fallen to $800 and unemployment, now at about 50 per cent is expected to grow to 70 per cent. Economic planning is frustrated if not pointless as Israeli permission to import raw materials and export produce can be withheld at any time with no notice.

We briefly visited both Shijai'a and Darraj Family Health Care Centre in Gaza City which are serving people in particularly over-crowded and under-served areas. There we also saw the mobile dental clinic van. Between the two centres, some 18,000 families are served through general health provision as well as ante- and post-natal care, well-baby clinics, family planning, and health education. We were told by the child psychiatrist present that one of the major health issues people face is stress related disorders. He told us that 70 per cent of all children and 76 per cent of young mothers were affected.

The NECC Boys' Vocational Training Centre is offering a three-year course for 14-16 year-olds in carpentry, furniture making, metal/aluminium work and welding programmes. Recent statistics show that this provides genuine job opportunities for young men who have dropped out of school. The employment rate one year after graduation for trainees is 95 per cent.

Mr Jabr Wishah of the Palestinian Centre for Human Rights told us of the continued human rights abuses perpetrated by the Israeli Defence Force, but also mentioned that the PCHR was also dealing with incidents involving the Palestinian Authority. The centre is in contact with Amnesty International and other international agencies. The premises of this organization were recently damaged when a bomb detonated in the building.

As it was impossible because of road closures to visit the south, the afternoon was spent travelling in the north of the Gaza Strip. Mr Munzer El Rayyes, a local citrus farmer and Chairman of the Agricultural Engineers Association came with us and shared some of the frustrations and economic implications of the recent closures. We first visited "Beach Camp" in Gaza City which, with more than 128,000 people, is the second largest refugee camp in the area. There we found ourselves, not for the first time, impaled on a sharp rhetorical hook: "*Groups like yours come to us*," cried an old lady, "*they look at us like animals in a zoo, but nothing ever changes.*"

We also visited a concrete factory that had recently been bulldozed by the Israeli Defence Forces together with the neighbouring private home. Although we saw beautiful citrus groves with trees heavy with fruit, we were told that the farmers cannot presently export these fruit, along with carnations, and other fruit and vegetables because the borders are closed. We found 16kg of oranges were available for one dollar!

Standing on a farm near the Netzarim crossroads where, caught in a photo which shocked the world, a young Palestinian boy was shot dead, we looked at the remains of mature olive and citrus groves, houses and factories, destroyed by the Israeli Defence Force in the name of "security". Away to our right a bulldozer was at work, clearing fields of tomatoes, cucumbers, and strawberries for 500 meters on either side of a road which had been commandeered to give "safe passage" to a small number of illegal settlers. Ahead of us their bus, accompanied by a heavily armed convoy made its solitary way along this road to Israel as warning shots rang out from a nearby watchtower. For the Palestinian population, however, no such travel is possible. The closure of the border has cut off workers from their jobs and wider families, produce from its markets, medical and other essential supplies from a situation of great and terrible need. Even within Gaza itself military checkpoints and harassment have transformed a journey of 40 minutes to one of several hours. "*Our big prison is now three small prisons,*" we were told.

Dr Haider Abdel Shafi, Chairman of the Gaza Red Crescent Society, who had been part of the Palestinian negotiation team in Madrid in the early 1990s, reminded us forcibly of British responsibility for what has happened to the Palestinians over the years. He also spoke of the inherent difficulties of the so-called 'Oslo Peace Process' e.g. in the omission of the question of Palestinian refugees and their right of return. We also had an interesting meeting with Dr Ziad Abu-Amr, Chairman of the Political Committee of the Palestinian Legislative Council, who spoke of the challenges and restrictions facing the Palestinian Authority, and of their journey towards more democratic structures. He also asked, "*What did (the Israelis) learn from their own terrible experience that they have to treat us in the same way?*"

At Ahli Arab Hospital we met the Director, Miss Suhaila Tarazi. The hospital is held in high regard in the community because of its excellent services, in spite of shortage of money and difficulties with the provision of supplies, due to the border closures. The Accident and Emergency Unit, with only four beds, is treating an incredible number of patients with very limited resources.

Lastly, we were able to speak with Mr Husam El-Nounou from the Gaza Community Mental Health Programme which offers not only individual and family counselling, but educates parents on helpful strategies to support their traumatised children. Due to economic pressures, as well as injuries, deaths and the stress of living under occupation in a very volatile situation, violence in the home is on the increase, as it is on the streets. The Gaza Community Mental Health Programme staff has found that 750,000 residents of Gaza have been imprisoned by the Israelis over the last 30 years, about 15 per cent of the population over that period. If children, women and elderly men are discounted, probably more than half of the young men have been imprisoned – and in prison, most have suffered physical and psychological abuse.

All this is happening because, as Mr El-Nounou put it, *"Israel has dehumanised the Palestinian, so your house can be demolished, your trees uprooted, your children killed because you are not equal to an Israeli, and anyway are less than human. The young fight so as to keep their personal dignity - because they have lost everything else."*

Thursday 22 March

The next morning was spent visiting the NECC Secretarial Studies Centre for young women, which offered a variety of courses - secretarial and computer training, English language. In the same building there is also available a sewing and dressmaking course, and a dressmaking and knitting income generating cooperative. These are measures to enable women, both married and unmarried, to acquire income-generating skills with which to support their families.

In one secretarial class an obviously intelligent young woman asked us: *"Do you regard us as terrorists?"* In that question were compressed a sense of frustration and despair, a feeling, encountered frequently, of Palestinians being second class and of little account, and a reminder of the power and importance of words and slogans in this land. The way in which it was asked reflected the amazing grace and dignity which was yet so evident in a people that has suffered so much.

We all found the visit to Gaza a deeply troubling experience. It was a rare case in which the facts do speak for themselves. The Palestinian stance towards Israel is ultimately determined by the experienced reality of living under occupation. The reality of "occupation" is that in a territory under the acknowledged jurisdiction of the Palestinian Authority, all aspects of economic and social life are subject to the decisions and the vetoes of the Government of Israel. In this way occupation slides into the reality of colonisation. An NGO official summed it up in words which identify the massive impediments to any genuine peace agreement, since genuine peace would require at least the beginnings of mutual trust and respect.

"There is an everyday message for all Palestinians. You are not equal to Israelis: your farm is not important and can be bulldozed, your olive trees are not important and can be uprooted, your children are not important and can be deprived of the chance of health and education."

In such a context it would be extraordinary if there were no outbreaks of Palestinian violence! Some, certainly, have been appalling, though in this region the violence can in no way threaten the security of the State of Israel. This violence draws massive counter measures. The clearances we watched serve also as collective punishment, to add to the rocket attacks and the helicopter gunships. Yet all such Palestinian violence is too readily termed 'terrorism', as if that were a one-way process, and regardless of the recognition that there is in international law a right to resist occupation, a right which the British and Irish churches have been ready to uphold elsewhere. On any sober calculation it is the Palestinians who are brought all too often to despair and even terror.

Galilee Diary
Wednesday 21 March 2001

CTBI group: Fred George, Christopher Gillham, Esther Hookway, John Waller

Leaving Jerusalem early, the four of us destined for Galilee were driven north up the main road that bypasses Ramallah and Nablus until we were stopped at an army checkpoint. Because of shooting ahead, all traffic was turned back and directed on to what was little more than a track running north beside the Jordanian border. We thus were late to arrive in Nazareth, there to be welcomed by Judge Khalil Aboud, Chairman of the International Christian Committee in Galilee. After introducing us to the centre of Nazareth and visiting the renovated, but virtually empty, souk and the Greek Orthodox Church and Latin Catholic Basilica, we began an intensive series of meetings.

Christian-Muslim Relations
Our first stop was the White Mosque. A brief introduction to Mr Atef El Fahoum informed us that he was the tenth trustee of the El Fahoum dynasty, which built the White Mosque in the eighteenth century. Mr El Fahoum and Judge Khalil had been friends since they were children.

"The message from the White Mosque is one of peace," said Mr El Fahoum. *"It is like an oasis in the desert."* *"The El Fahoums are one of the oldest Muslim families in this town, keeping the tradition of peace and cooperation,"* Judge Khalil interjected. *"But now there is a big difference between Islam and the Muslims,"* Mr El Fahoum continued. *"The Muslims here are the Orthodox Sunni."* Mr El Fahoum seemed to represent a more liberal strand of Islam, commenting on the more revolutionary inclinations of the younger generation for whom religion was a tool to gain political importance in their own community. He went on to mention the 'Shab Hadin' controversy in Nazareth, a dispute over a piece of land, claimed to be religious land by fundamentalist Muslims, and hence a proposed site for a mosque. The Israeli Government had given its permission, and plans exist for a large mosque with seven minarets to be built directly in front of the Catholic Basilica of the Annunciation in downtown Nazareth – the biggest Christian church in the whole of the Middle East. We walked past the site and saw the newly laid corner stone. *"The Israelis give money to the fundamentalists in an attempt to foster bad relations between the Muslims and the Christians,"* Mr El Fahoum concluded. This point was also made by Mr Nagib Rizik, former Deputy Mayor of Nazareth – that the government supported the growth of fundamentalism in order to divide and rule.

After a late lunch we embarked on a series of meetings at the ICC offices arranged by Judge Aboud:

Educator for the future
Fr Elias Chacour, the author of **Blood Brothers**, came originally from the Christian village of Bharm, destroyed in 1951. Fr Elias was on his way to the airport to fly to Japan to collect a $300,000 peace prize, which will go towards the Mar Elias educational complex which he has established at Ibillin. *"We do not wish to continue attending the Jewish University as foreigners in our own land,"* he explained. His plan is to build an Arab-Israeli Christian university in Galilee, as a bridge between Israel and the surrounding Arab countries, when peace finally comes. This university is already at the advanced planning stage and good contact with several American universities promises a sound accreditation and an agreement for partnership. The complex includes a high school, with 57 per cent Muslim students and the rest Christian, and 28 Jews on the staff. *"Our mission here [in Israel] is to give an authentic witness to the Jews and Muslims; we do not want to proselytize,"* Fr Elias told us. As he got up to leave he concluded, *"Make the story [of the Palestinian plight] known to the outside world, and get as many Jewish citizens as allies as you can...we do not have any hope in your governments, our only hope comes from the Church."*

The Baptists and the Orthodox

Fr Elias left to catch his plane, and Mr Fuad Haddad, Principal of the Baptist School, and Pastor Philip Sa'ad, Chairman of the Baptist Association of Israel, took his place. There are some 900 to 1000 Baptist households in the country, we were told, most of which come from other Christian backgrounds. As well as eighteen churches, there is a Conference Centre in Tel Aviv and a school in Nazareth. Even Judge Khalil, Greek Orthodox himself and sceptical of the motives of converts to the Baptist Church, had to admit that this was one of the best Arab schools in the country. The Baptist mission had began early in the twentieth century, helped by missionaries from the Southern United States in the 1960s, and their first church in the Holy Land had been in Nazareth.

Mr Fuad Farah, Chairman of the Orthodox National Council, and Director of the Nazareth YMCA, whom we met later on in the afternoon reminded us, *"Orthodox Christians have been here for two thousand years. It was from here that Christianity spread throughout the world."* Frustrations on the part of the Orthodox Christians over the proselytising activity of 'new' Christian churches was compounded by a perceived lack of support and spiritual leadership towards their flock, on the part of the Orthodox Church hierarchy. *"The problem is not with the Greeks as such,"* Judge Khalil interjected, *"but simply the fact that they do not know the needs of the local communities."* He expressed concern over the fact that the Orthodox Church of the Assumption – where the Virgin is said to have been greeted by Gabriel – only holds 250 people and a new church in Nazareth is urgently needed. There is an Orthodox community of 17,000 in Nazareth. Furthermore, there are no trained catechists, no young men coming forward to be trained for the priesthood, and no liturgical books or catechetical material are available.

We were already aware that the Ancient Churches in the Middle East were critical of the Protestant Evangelical Churches whose zeal to preach the Gospel did not always taken into consideration the local context, nor recognize the contradiction in 'converting the converted'. The Orthodox understanding on mission is based on *being* rather than *doing*. Being a *witness* to the faith is a *missionary* responsibility.

As it is, Christians (of all denominations) are already a minority within the Palestinian minority. Now, according to Mr Farah's estimation Christians make up one per cent of the population in Israel, three per cent of the population in Iraq and 10 per cent of the population in Syria. The overall contribution and influence of the Christian population is further diminished by the fact that they are scattered all over the country. This means that on an electoral level they can have no impact either. Mr Farah accepts the prediction that in twenty five years time there will be no Christians left in Israel.

Adalah, the Legal Centre for Arab Minority Human Rights

We moved on from church matters to discuss issues of human rights. Hassan Jabbarin from Adalah, the Legal Centre for Arab Minority Human Rights, was only able to give us a few minutes of his time, on his way back to Jerusalem. There, two Israeli police officers were being tried for using live ammunition on Palestinians during rioting on 8 October 2000, sparked off by the descent of hundreds of Jewish residents from Nazareth Illit into the old Arab town of Nazareth. Thirteen Palestinians had been shot dead.

Mr Jabbarin explained that Adalah was representing the families of the Palestinian victims before the 'Commission of Inquiry' (COI) set up in November 2000 by Ehud Barak "to investigate the clashes which involved security forces and Arab and Jewish citizens of Israel" in October 2000. Adalah has challenged the mandate of the Commission on several points and views the appropriate mandate for the COI to be "the investigation of the killing of thirteen Arab Palestinian citizens and the wounding of hundreds more by security forces during the October 2000 demonstrations."

Mr Jabbarin told us that, despite the pending court order against them, the officers in question had remained on duty since the October events and still had the full support of the Chief Commander of the Police behind them. *"You would suspend the police in Britain, or rather, the police themselves would have suspended them!"* one of our group said. Riots had just broken out in the Jerusalem courtroom as Mr Jabbarin was on his way to meet us. The families of the Palestinians shot dead had tried to attack the police officers when they admitted using snipers and live ammunition. Mr Jabbarin was going to file a petition to get the proceedings suspended and the officers suspended from duty.

Thursday 22 March

Bishop under fire

The next morning we followed Judge Khalil to the Latin Catholic Bishopric to meet the Italian-born bishop, Rt. Revd Boulos Marcuzzo. As we sat over our coffee and pistachios we listened to his account of a recent incident in which he, a nun and a young man, travelling in a diplomatic car with a church flag, had been stopped on the road. On being ordered out of the car, they were shot at by an Israeli solider 15 metres away. *"He obviously didn't shoot to kill,"* the bishop explained, *"as he could easily have done that, being so close."* In reflecting upon the incident the bishop was not seeking to illustrate what a close shave he had just had with death, but rather to point out that if he, with his diplomatic immunity, is subject to this ill-treatment, all the more so are Palestinians, who lack any kind of protection. The twist in the tale was that two days after the incident an Israeli official visited the bishopric to offer a formal apology. The calm and collected way in which the bishop spoke was an example of real Christian witness and love. Like many of the other inspiring church leaders whom we met during our trip to the Middle East, here was yet another whose life was on the line daily. But for as long as there were people to minister to, he would be there to support and encourage them in the struggle of their daily lives.

"Future perspectives? I see the situation as very black," said Bishop Marcuzzo with conviction. *"Is it possible in the third millennium to have the oldest people in the world with no rights?"* he asked us. *"Some 47 per cent of the population have not even got two dollars a day to live on. Suffering brings despair, and despair leads to disorder. In Nazareth,"* he went on to say, *"the Arabs are fighting for equality; in the West Bank they are fighting for a state."*

One of our group asked the bishop whether he thought that an extreme right-wing government could deliver more than a progressive one, as had been done in the past. *"You have to be a De Gaulle or a Churchill to do that!"* he retorted with a smile. *"Sharon was exalted in the US. Where is the pressure from the other sides? There is none! Why is Europe doing nothing? This is something I have to ask you."* After a pause, he concluded. *"Europe is nothing."*

Women Against Violence

We retraced our steps down the narrow streets to the ICC, already late for our next rendezvous with Aida Suleiman from "Women Against Violence", a Palestinian NGO. "Women against Violence" have a huge and varied agenda. Founded in 1992, it operates two shelters staffed by Arab women for Arab women. Aida was one of the seven founding members who, realizing that gender-based violence was a taboo subject, that nothing was being done about it and that the majority even legitimised it, felt convinced that concrete action was needed. The main aims of the organization are to expose problems and raise awareness, to establish services for women survivors and to effect social change by promoting the status of women. Aida explained that although patriarchal societies exist all over the world, the problem here is that the Palestinian Arabs are already a minority suffering discrimination, and within this minority the women suffer further discrimination. The organization does a lot of work with the Arab Bedouin women of the Negev who represent approximately 12 per cent of the Arab minority in Israel. There are around 110,000 Bedouins in the Negev today, half of whom live in the poorest localities recognized by Israel, and the other half in villages which are not recognized at all. Denied any form of basic service, they are unable to build or develop their communities in any way.

Aida told us the recent story of a Bedouin girl who, on suspicion of having relations with a neighbouring boy, had been buried alive together with him. She had managed to stay alive for some time, thanks to a small pocket of air, and then finally she broke free. She now suffers from trauma and acute claustrophobia but has since been obliged to marry one of the men responsible for burying her in the first place. It was either this, or living with a death threat for the rest of her life. The girl's only wish was that her husband died early, or at least lost interest in her quickly.

Land Confiscation
We glided up towards the Jewish suburb of Nazareth Illit in one of the stretch limousines that serve as taxis in Israel-Palestine only to break down when we got to the top. These were our last few hours in Galilee. Our guide, Mohammed Zeidan from the Arab Association of Human Rights, took us over to the edge of a road nearby which gave us a birds-eye view of the whole Galilee area, Arab Nazareth below and some other clusters of houses and villages dotted over hill tops and in valleys. While waiting for our 'rescue' he gave us a clear picture of the Israeli planning strategy for the Judaisation of Galilee using the "live map" in front of our eyes.

We could see as far as the ruined town of Safforyi, empty of its Arab inhabitants since their eviction in the 1948 war, and most of whom now lived 2 km away in Nazareth. Evacuees of this kind have a peculiar, almost Orwellian status, of "present absentees". There are 20,000 "present absentees" in Israel, – Palestinians who live in Israel but are not permitted to return to their homes. Safforyi is now a Jewish kibbutz called "Zeppori".

The town of Reineh was also visible. Land around it had been confiscated and a by-pass had been built (route 74). Such roads have the dual purpose of connecting Jewish settlements to each other without crossing neighbouring Arab towns, and of halting any further growth of the Arab town.

There are no green areas in Nazareth at all, but on the north side we could see what looked like a small wood or copse. This was a green area belonging to Nazareth, Mr Zeidan explained, but it was confiscated by Israel for use as army headquarters. Recently however, the land had begun to be developed for tourism by the Israelis but the municipality of Nazareth is struggling to reclaim it. Apparently there are 36 different laws by which Arab land can be expropriated. The majority are for "public purposes", which are usually Jewish. Out of 1200 dunums confiscated in Nazareth, 80 had been used for public buildings and the rest for Jewish housing and for "military" or "security" purposes.

Nazareth Illit is certainly a well-appointed and comfortable Jewish suburb standing in stark contrast to the cramped and poorly served city of Nazareth below. But then there are only 14,200 dunums for 60,000 people in Arab Nazareth and 34,000 dunums for 45,000 people in Nazareth Illit – so this explains why – there is 5.5 times more space up there.

Our new taxi hailed us from across the road and we drove off. Mr Zeidan wanted to take us past the Arab town of Eln Meil, to the east of Nazareth Illit. Cultivated land and olive groves surrounded Eln Meil. The Israeli Government had confiscated all the land for "public purposes", Mr Zeidan told us. As we drove closer we saw a bulldozer digging up the earth around the edge of the village – right up to the statutory three-metre limit from the houses.

"This was my father's land." On the way back down to Nazareth Mr Zeidan points up to the trees. *"He inherited the land from my grandfather who inherited it from his father and so on."* It was confiscated in 1976 during the controversial and violent Israeli land confiscation programme, which led to a number of Palestinians being killed.

Losing their land has led to a significant social change for the Palestinian people, for whom agriculture had been a way of life for centuries. Many former Arab farmers are forced to earn their living as unskilled labourers in the Jewish industrial areas and (to add insult to injury) these Jewish industrial areas are being built on the Arab confiscated land!

Returning down to old Nazareth, we picked up our things from the ICC office, said goodbye to Judge Khalil and got into another taxi. We were silent for most of the four-hour drive back to Jerusalem – each with our own thoughts, trying to hold together in one the narratives we had heard and trying to find the truth in each of them. It was an intensive two days of new faces, of new facts, of new evidence of the Arab Israelis' struggle against discrimination and inequality and of the plight of the remaining Christians in that troubled land.

West Bank Diary
Wednesday 21 March

CTBI group: Robert Davidson, Gillian Kingston, Charles Reed, Paul Renshaw

Travelling to Hebron along the notorious Road 60 was an eye-opening experience. We passed a number of settlements and noted the swathes of arable land on either side of the road, confiscated and cleared as a security measure. We were told of olive groves which had been cleared to make way for settlements, and of settlements which were only semi-occupied as the owners of many of the apartments were living out of the country. We had been told categorically by Avi Granot that *"The question of settlements is irrelevant"* and that no new settlements would be established in the West Bank and Gaza. He had refused to be drawn on the issues of the expansion of existing settlements, saying that such expansion was "natural". Looking at the settlements as we passed, we could see how they were being sited round Jerusalem, in what appears to be an effort to surround the city and create more "facts on the ground" which will inevitably prove another hurdle for any peace process.

The first stop was at the headquarters of the Temporary International Presence in Hebron. TIPH is currently made up of personnel from Denmark, Sweden, Norway, Switzerland, Turkey and Italy. Their role is strictly limited to "observation". TIPH only functions in the city of Hebron itself. The Jewish settlement of Kiryat Arba, for example, is outside its area. TIPH divides Hebron into two areas, H1 and H2, corresponding to the A and B security areas. TIPH is received favourably, in broad terms, by the Palestinian community, rather less so by the settlers, but this varies according to the interpretation of events.

The research officer, Jens Kirk Neilsen, a Danish university lecturer in Middle East Studies with some Arabic, briefed us on the history of Hebron and showed us, on detailed maps, the location of the settlements and of the major flashpoints in the area. Then we proceeded in two cars to tour the area, seeing flashpoints familiar from television newscasts. We viewed a small city centre settlement, for the security of which the wholesale fruit and vegetable market had been closed down along with part of the retail market. We also saw the Ibrahimi Mosque in which 29 Muslim worshippers had been killed by Baruch Goldstein in 1994. It was in the aftermath of this atrocity that TIPH came into being. As we passed back towards the Headquarters, we noticed tyres burning at one checkpoint and our Italian driver looked up at a sentry point and accelerated, *"They are expecting something to happen,"* he said.

Leaving Hebron, we travelled back to Bethlehem, where we went to see the Church of the Nativity, empty except for a group of German tourists, silent except for their singing. No pushing, no queuing, no manoeuvring to get a photograph…. eerie, if one had been there before. In the place of the Incarnation, we considered the present oppressors, the present massacre of the Innocents, the present injustice.

We lunched with Viola Raheb and an American friend. Viola is an articulate, committed, young Lutheran woman who is in charge of the education programme of the Lutheran Church in Israel/Palestine and Jordan. Though the headquarters of the church is in Jerusalem, she has to operate from Bethlehem as she has been refused a travel pass to go to Jerusalem. 'Headhunted' from as far away as Germany, she is not permitted to travel in her own country. She spoke, among other things, about the role that Palestinian civil society organizations play and the debate on a Palestinian constitution which some Christians feared would have too strong an Islamic flavour.

After lunch, we spent time with her brother, the Revd Dr Mitri Raheb, at The International Centre of Bethlehem. A Lutheran minister, concerned to contextualize the reading of the Bible, he spoke of a number of challenges presented by the Intifada. One was pastoral and revolved around the issue and experience of psychological stress. Another was the use of violence. A large number of young people had been killed in this Intifada. *"Dying,"* he suggested, *"does not solve anything!"* The importance of war and instability in some of the Biblical texts presents theological problems. *"We lack the power to transform the enemy into the neighbour."*

There is, he felt, also a sense of helplessness in the Palestinian Christian community. This is a paradox because without peace with the Palestinians, Israeli security cannot be achieved. Nevertheless, there are many new issues for Palestinian Christians to address, not least that of trying to be part of an inclusive society which can deal with the demands of religious pluralism and the role of Christians within an Islamic milieu. Taking forward these issues requires Christians to critique their own theological heritage and their cultural and national myths. *"Critique is part of witness".*

Viola accompanied us on a visit to Beit Jala, where we saw the shattered buildings, homes to Palestinian extended families, rendered uninhabitable by shelling from Gilo on the other side of the valley. We saw the façade of a home in which a young boy had been killed, and we thought of the cynical manner in which we had been told earlier in the week that the Israeli army had the power to ascertain whether people were present or not before they fired.

On then to Aida refugee camp, housing 1948 refugees from the coastal towns. There we were met by Dr AbdelFattah Abu-Srour, a Paris-trained microbiologist, who, with his wife, had come back to work alongside his own people. We were deeply challenged by what we saw and by some of the things which were said to us, not least the unanswerable claim, *"It isn't for us to pay the price for what others have done".*

An old man said to some of us, *"We don't want just visitors",* clearly implying that those who come and see must go back and tell. We were reminded yet again of the double standards which exist in Western perceptions of what is happening in Israel/Palestine, *"When the French fought the Germans, they were the 'resistance': when we fight the Jews, we are 'terrorists'. When a Jew is killed, the President of the US sends his condolences; when a Palestinian is killed, it is as if it never happened."*

We diffidently entered a home which had been badly damaged by fire from Gilo. The trees in between the gun emplacement and the camp had been trimmed to allow a better view of the 'target'. Children ran around through the broken glass and one little tot had some bullets in her hands. As we stood in the corridor, to the right was normality, a regular untidy family bedroom, with photographs of a wedding, personal effects and so on; to the left, the blackened shell of what had been a sitting room. In one room, we saw how bullets had penetrated the room, gone through the closed door and embedded themselves in the wall of the corridor.

Perhaps the most moving encounter of many moving encounters was with a group of children involved in the Al-Rowaad (Pioneers) theatre group. They were practising as we arrived, but made us welcome and sang songs for us from their forthcoming production. In their drama, they and their leaders enact the drama going on outside and try to come to some sort of terms with it. Their bright faces come to mind as we listen to the news since we have been there....what have they suffered, if not physically, certainly emotionally and mentally in the meantime?

We bade farewell to Dr AbdelFattah. *"It's been a good day,"* he said, *"no-one's been killed."*

As darkness had come, we had to be taken to a checkpoint on the road below the Tantur Ecumenical Institute. We walked through to the other side and almost immediately found a sheroot back to Jerusalem. Others, those with whom we had spent the day, were obliged to stay behind. They had not the freedom to offer us the courtesy of a drive back to Notre Dame.

Jerusalem Diary
Thursday, 22 March

CTBI group: Robert Davidson, Gillian Kingston, Charles Reed, Paul Renshaw

Another early morning encounter with the world of diplomats, this time at the British Consulate-General in Sheikh Jarrah. Here we met with Robin Kealy (British Consul-General), Isolde Moylan (Irish Representative to the Palestinian Authority), Catherina Hempel Kipp (Swedish Consul General) and Jean Breteche (Representative of the European Commission).

Conversation focussed on the contribution, real and possible, of the European Union to the political dynamic in Israel/Palestine. However, Common Foreign and Security Policy demands cooperation among 15 countries, and in controversial matters the finding of consensus can be tricky and time-consuming. Another inbuilt difficulty is that for each member country, there may be a discrepancy between "on the ground" observation and the stance of its capital.

The discussion covered whether there had been a real possibility of agreement between the Israeli and Palestinian sides at Taba and the need for "a road map for progress" out of a situation of frustration, desperation and humiliation. Reference was made to the Gaza situation, where some Israeli soldiers were quoted as saying that *"We don't want to be here"* – a small sign of hope.

Overall, we sensed from this diplomatic conversation a deep concern for the whole situation, but a certain powerlessness to do anything much about it.

From there to the headquarters of Sabeel, where we were received by the Revd Canon Naim Ateek and members of the Board. Sabeel, in the words of its Purpose Statement, is "*an ecumenical grassroots liberation theology movement among Palestinian Christians which encourages women, men, and youth to discern what God is saying to them as their faith connects with the hard realities of their daily life: occupation, violence, discrimination and human rights violations.*" The word is Arabic for "the way", and can also mean "a channel" or "spring" of life-giving water.

In a book-lined office, we listened to a group of highly articulate and cultured people speak of the constant humiliations to which they are subjected as Palestinians. "*You are free to travel in my country, I am not!*" said Jean Zaru, Vice President of Sabeel and Presiding Clerk of the Ramallah Society of Friends.

We heard that, in the view of Sabeel, there seems to be no strategy on the part of the churches for dealing with diminishing numbers, with '*more attention to internal sheep-stealing than to loss to Islam'*. The influence of the Christian community, as long as it lasts, is stronger than its numbers would suggest, and educated Muslims would miss its presence. Uneducated Muslims, on the other hand, are unaware of a Christian presence or else shocked that *real* Palestinians can be Christian!

History rears its ugly head....Christians were seen as indigenous until colonial times, after which they were often perceived as "coming from outside". *"Imported Christianity has split us!"* There is a perception that some churches are loyal to a leadership abroad. Yasser Arafat, however, is insisting on Christian representation, and many of the Intifada songs reflect an appreciation of pluralism. Minorities are the *"embroidery which brings colour to the cloth".* However, the water is muddied by the presence of Christian Zionist organizations. Many people are unable to differentiate between one expression of Christianity and another. (This was a theme we heard on a number of occasions from a variety of groups.)

"Have our friends failed us?" A shocking question, but we listened as the group expressed their (strong) opinion that the West has a guilt complex with regard to Israel...the Holocaust must not be allowed to happen again. Even the mainline churches seem to have a psychological block which prevents clear, forceful, prophetic criticism of the State of Israel. Thus, *"in the name of security, they get away with murder".* Words like balance and neutrality are often used. *"But,"* we were asked, *"how can we have balance between justice and injustice? There is a conflict because of imbalance."* These are hard sayings, but, as one of the group pointed out, *"If it is difficult for you to hear it, think how difficult it is for me to live through it."*

We asked what we could do on return:
- produce a full report
- monitor the situation and make responses to injustice
- challenge Jewish leaders in Britain and Ireland when they appear to silence the truth
- CTBI might consider the possibility of bringing a Jewish delegation
- establish a standing group to make regular representation to the Foreign and Commonwealth Office

It was fitting that we were able to go from this troubling and forthright conversation to the chapel, and gather round the table of the Lord to share bread and wine, the body broken and the blood shed...for us all.

In the afternoon, we met with Mr Azmi Bishara, a prominent Arab member of the Knesset, candidate for Prime Minister in 1999 and political pragmatist, who believed that, in the last analysis, interests are more powerful than "political theology".

Azmi Bishara outlined his perception of the factors contributing to the change of Israeli regime. Ehud Barak found himself in a conflict position on all sides, with his own party, with secular forces in Israel and with the religious parties. The Palestinians expected from him what they had not got from Netanyahu. The Israelis wanted peace and security. Each was disappointed. He was adamant that Sharon's government would last its full term and believed it should certainly be treated in that light. (We had heard another perception elsewhere.) He believed that a role for the EU was unrealistic. *"Europeans gave up power in 1956."*

Responding to a question on the influence and money of Arabs outside the area, he pointed out that Arabs have, on the whole, become more integrated in the societies they adopt than have Zionists. Pinochet's government, he pointed out, had four ex-Palestinian ministers!

Reunited with the rest of the team, we met with an impressive group of politically liberal Jews from different traditions in Judaism and involved in different areas of reconciliation work - Yehezkel Landau (a peace educator), Debbie Weizmann (a teacher trainer) and Rabbi Arik Aschermann (Director of Rabbis for Human Rights). It was painful to listen to them agonizing over the injustices which their state is perpetrating on its Palestinians neighbours and Arab citizens.

Arik Aschermann, American-born and brought up to believe that a basic part of what it means to be a Jew is to be concerned with universal human rights and social justice, explained that the situation required the peace movement to move "from protest to non-violent resistance". He told us of a group who were going out the following day to the village of Rantis, north of Ramallah, to fill in some of the trenches dug by the IDF to prevent the free movement of Palestinians. *"These measures* (closures) *cannot be justified even in the name of security."* Water is another focus for discriminatory action, and we heard of places where Arabs have only two hours' water a week, while neighbouring Israelis have running water and swimming pools. It was pointed out that many Israelis would claim to be unaware of what is being done in their name, *"If I read only Israeli media, I might dismiss the Arabs too"*.

Yehezkel Landau declared himself to be *"a religious Zionist"*. He confessed that *"It is easier to take the Jews out of exile than to take the sense of exile out of Jews"*. On the land issue his position was that *"the land does not belong to us Jews: we belong to the land, as do Christians and Muslims"*. He acknowledged that to solve a global injustice against the Jews, the Palestinians had been asked to pay the price. Calling for a "priestly praxis of reconciliation" involving sacrifice, he observed that the meaning of sacrifice is to make sacred by renunciation. Might Israel be called to make both power and land sacred in this way?

Yehezkel told us briefly the story behind the "Open House" project in Ramle. We heard of a house confiscated from Palestinians in 1947 and given to a Jewish Bulgarian couple who eventually became his parents-in-law. Years later, members of the Palestinian family returned and asked if they might look around the house. This was the beginning of a creative and prophetic association, through which the Open House now serves the needs of Arab children from Ramle, with Christian, Jewish and Muslim involvement..

Dai-Lakibbush- End the Occupation

"The significance of this demonstration is that it will be the first time that Jewish peace organizations have moved from passive protest to active resistance. The aim is to target the policy of the government done in our name. Those of you who want to be arrested will certainly have an opportunity to do so, but remember this is a non violent demonstration." It was in this manner that Rabbi Arik Aschermann rallied some 300 peace activists who had assembled in the car park behind the King David Hotel, Jerusalem on Friday 23 March, on the do's and don'ts of civil resistance.

The focus of the day's activities was the village of Rantis, near Ramallah. Rantis with a population of 3,000, had been under siege by the Israeli Defence Force (IDF) for six months. The village is totally cut off from other Palestinian areas in the West Bank. It has no doctor and no medical care. The "closure" has brought high unemployment with farmers denied access to the surrounding land. The deep trenches that scar the approach roads to and from Rantis and the presence of Israeli Defence Forces with their guns targetted on out-skirting farmhouses is indicative of the siege mentality that has gripped Israel since the start of the Al-Aqsa Intifada.

/cont

The decision to target Rantis and physically fill in the trench in order to make the road passable was taken by some 15 peace organizations. Despite the number of organizations involved there was little doubt as to the fragility of the Israeli peace camp. Jeff Halper (Committee Against House Demolitions) pointed out: *"The Israeli peace wing is fragmented and divided as to what is actually meant by 'peace', but demonstrations and acts of civil resistance like this encourages organizations to work together."*

Miriam Keren, a 63 year old retired geography teacher from Tel Aviv, elaborated the point. *"I am active in four peace organizations but the peace organizations are not very active. I think Sharon has changed, but I still don't know how far. I am hoping that today's actions will encourage him to change a little further."* According to Nathan Musselman, a student from the Applied Research Institute in Jerusalem, *"Our small numbers prevent action but being neutral is no longer an option".*

At one level the sight of 300-odd people, most of them senior citizens on their hands and knees physically clawing at the earth was deeply moving. At another level their actions appeared frustratingly pathetic and I am still unsure what was achieved beyond the purely symbolic. Yes, the demonstrations achieved their goal of making the road passable, but according to one report, two hours after the event bulldozers arrived to dig out fresh trenches. In addition the army has made the "apartheid system" between Palestinians and Israelis more visible by placing large concrete slabs in front of the trenches.

And yet in the midst of all the day's activity I was left with the distinct impression that something important had taken place. At a very simple level a dialogue had occurred between Palestinians, Israeli peace activists, and members of the IDF. There was, for instance, a real poignancy in seeing local Palestinians handing out "American Cola" to 300 human bulldozers working under the midday sun. At the same time hearing an army reservist say that he would prefer to be helping the demonstrators rather than policing them was an important comment for all sides to hear. All too often the Arab-Israel conflict is painted in black and white terms without acknowledging the complex shades of grey that exist in between. Rantis was a good example of both the diversity and fragility of views that exist within Israel/Palestine.

CR

Yehezkel also insisted that *"Truth telling is part of the process of reconciliation".* The fact that more than 400 Palestinian villages had been erased completely from the map of Israel is an injustice which must be acknowledged, suggesting that an action such as placing plaques at the sites of these villages may be a part of a litany of reconciliation leading to healing.

Meeting the Patriarchs
Our time in the Holy Land concluded with three meetings at the Greek Orthodox, Armenian Apostolic and Latin Patriarchates, on 22 and 23 March.

Metropolitan Cornelius, the Greek Orthodox Locum Tenens since the death of Patriarch Diodorus, left us with the memorable phrase, *"Delegations come, delegations go, nothing ever changes".* HB Patriarch Torkum Manoogian left us in no doubt of his astonishment and dismay on hearing of Ehud Barak's Camp David proposal that the Armenian Quarter come under Jewish jurisdiction while the Christian and Muslim Quarters fall under the Palestinian Authority.

The Latin Catholic Patriarch, HB Michel Sabbah, in our last meeting, gave us several succinct messages, *"Your coming is very good. We need new action, but the question is 'what?' You/we need to give the right image of the situation, i.e. that of (our) living under military occupation. This must be ended. It is not the image given in the media - 'Israel good, Palestinians bad - and with no esteem for life'."*

Patriarch Sabbah was clear that the occupation is the primary violence. The Palestinians are a people under servitude and their violence is a response to this condition. Over Jerusalem he said that Israeli national pride gets in the way. *"They need to recognize in principle that Jerusalem was occupied and should be returned - then issues of shared sovereignty can be discussed. For Palestinians Jerusalem must be an open city: it cannot be hostage to security measures. 'Shared sovereignty' ought to be the way forward."*

On the Right to Return, there is a need to recognize principles and then discuss how to implement them. Israeli's denial of responsibility is wrong. He acknowledged that, physically, all the Palestinian refugees could not go back to their original homes.

Patriarch Sabbah was under no illusion about the current realities. The Israelis want a *"racist, religious state".* He noted, however, that they already have one million Arab citizens and, because of fears of the demographic implications, they prefer to be in *"a situation of struggle".* In this situation *"our citizens are not protected. Israeli security, not the PA, is really, in charge. Closures are like living in a large prison. "*

Patriarch Sabbah called for "the prophetic voice" to be raised. Governments cannot be allowed to ignore individuals and think only in terms of "interests, structures and games". *"Injustice for Palestinians cannot mean security for Israel. Security for Israel entails justice for the Palestinians. "*He acknowledged that a prophet could become a martyr but continued, *"so what, if it is for the community?"*

Despite the weaknesses of the churches, Patriarch Sabbah, echoing Bishop Munib, believed they have important roles as "agents of reconciliation". While relations with Muslim leaders were, he said, *"normal",* because of the shared Palestinian vision, they *"cannot join us in how to see an enemy - to love even in the face of aggression".* It is the calling of Palestinian Christians to be witnesses to Jesus Christ in a Muslim society. *"We are Arabs, part of Muslim society".* *"Our vocation is to be here with them, so I may have to find my way in a bad situation. "*In Patriarch Sabbah's view Islamic forces could find it difficult to exert real influence because of the international focus on the Middle East. He also cautioned us on political manipulation of Christian-Muslim relations, which sometimes makes interpretation difficult, even in the Christian-Christian sphere.

Saturday 24 March

With our afternoon departure from Tel Aviv the mission ended - feelings stirred, understanding deepened and many questions remaining. The hospitality of our Christian brothers and sisters in the Middle East had left its mark. So had the commitment of those we had met for whom the interwoven quests for peace with justice, human rights and the reconciliation of peoples are none other than a Gospel imperative.

Our visit had deliberately been to "the Middle East" and not just to Israel and the Occupied Territories. We had glimpsed a little of the life of the churches in four neighbouring Arab states, each exhibiting a unique interplay of political, economic, social, cultural and religious forces. Islam was, of course, virtually everywhere, in varying shades of green – the visit dispelled any tendency to think of it in monolithic terms. Our prayers for Christians making their life journey within a largely Islamic milieu were greatly enlivened. Perceptions of the roles of Britain and Ireland, past, present and future, provided us with much food for thought.

At the heart of the inability of the Middle East to become a region at ease with itself is, however, the Israel-Palestine crisis. It destabilises regional peace prospects and takes the lives of ordinary people, most of them Palestinian.

On the day of our leaving the Heads of the Jerusalem Churches issued a joint appeal out of their concern "for the spiritual, mental and bodily well-being of all the citizens of this Holy Land, Christian, Moslem and Jew....."

They expressed their conviction that "peace-seeking negotiations between the Israelis and the Palestinians are the only assured way of providing for the well being of all our peoples". "...the violence which has intensified over these past months will only end when both parties in the conflict make a determined effort to respect each other's rights while affirming the dignity and worth of every human life (man, woman and child)." They then "respectfully" requested "protection for all our people in order to assist the re-establishment of mutual trust and security for Israeli and Palestinian"...and called on "all peace-loving people from around the world to come and join us in a manifestation of just peace".

We were not to have known it, but our visit had taken place in a sort of lull before the Israel-Palestine struggle entered an even more dangerous and tragic storm. April was to see the use of F16s by the Israelis and May witnessed the appalling suicide bomb in Tel Aviv which claimed 20 young Israeli lives. The Jerusalem Church Leaders' Appeal remains to be answered.....

Too often we heard the words "nothing ever changes". For those who believe that "the grace (and truth) of God has dawned upon the world with healing for all", this must not be so.

Let Justice Flow- an evangelical reflection on a week in the Holy Land

The bus topped the brow of a hill and there before us lay the Jordan Valley. We were on Mount Nebo, near to the spot where Moses had gazed into the misty distance as he dreamed of the future of his people.

"The Promised Land!" proclaimed our Jordanian guide. In indignation, his Palestinian companion burst out, "It's not their promised land. It's our land!"

How one sympathized with her! But at least in part, she was wrong. There are few Evangelical Christians who would question the fact that the Jews are God's chosen people and that Moses was shown the Promised Land. But one may question for what it was promised and for what they were chosen.

Being chosen involves responsibilities as well as rights. Through the Prophet Amos, God proclaims those responsibilities, "Let justice flow like a stream, and righteousness like a river that never goes dry."

In modern Israel the river has gone dry and the stream does not flow. Rather, injustice is enshrined in the law and the very fabric of society. At every point of our visit, we saw injustice and the flouting of human dignity.

Where was justice when Israel permitted, indeed encouraged, foul tortures and the incarceration of prisoners in cells no bigger than broom cupboards in the South Lebanon prison of al-Khiam?
Where is justice when Palestinian villages are put under medieval siege as a mass punishment?

Where is justice when planning laws are used to confiscate Arab lands in order to transfer them to Jewish use?
Where is justice when the world's press laments over the awful murder of a Jewish baby by a Palestinian gunman, while the equally terrible murder of a Palestinian child by a Jewish settler goes totally unreported?
Where is justice when an Israeli Government official says that if one building is left standing in Beit Jala, Israel is showing commendable restraint?
Where is justice when people who fled before an invasion are denied either a right of return or compensation?
Where is justice when the victorious try to take from the vanquished even that little which is left to them?

Oh Amos, how your people need to learn from you of the road of righteousness prepared for God's chosen ones!

CG

Chapter 5

Christian Presence in the Middle East

1. Christianity and the Islamic milieu

In Middle Eastern church circles the very articulation of the term "Christian Presence" more than hints at its endangered nature within a generally Islamic environment. Christian emigration is a cause of great concern, particularly in Palestine, Jordan and Lebanon. There is more, however, to "Christian Presence" than mere numbers.

Christians in the Middle East have, for centuries, needed to live with and, indeed, under Islam. In the words of Bishop Kenneth Cragg, *"The high disdain Muslims had for the faith they invaded has been a permanent circumstance attending Arab Christianity."*[11] In these circumstances a centuries-long " survival game" has had to be played out by Middle Eastern Christians, at no little cost.

In 637AD the Patriarch Sophronius surrendered Jerusalem to the Caliph 'Umar. About 50 years later the Dome of the Rock was built on the site of Solomon's Temple, the building of which involved the use of Christian artisans and craftsmen from Constantinople. All this amounted to giving divided Christianity a clear sign that, to the Muslim way of thinking, its supersession was under way.[12]

After the Islamic conquest a minority status was imposed on Christianity. Christians (and Jews) became "dhimmis". In exchange for paying more taxes, official protection was afforded to such communities. They had certain defined privileges which allowed them to continue to worship in their own church buildings, and have ordained ministers and priests. Christians could not build new churches and often had to seek permission to repair existing ones. They could not bear arms and, historically, could not join the military. At one point Christians could only wear certain colours, which excluded the "Muslim" white. They were allowed to look after certain civil affairs in their own courts but they had to accept restricted freedoms, including on evangelism. This is one of the reasons why Christianity did not experience any growth in the area, and why new Churches have grown out of existing ones, thus undermining Christian solidarity and encouraging ecclesiastical fragmentation. Anyone was welcome to convert to Islam

---

11 Bishop Kenneth Cragg: The Arab Christian, Mowbray 1991, p.17
12 Cragg p.53

but the reverse was considered a crime punishable by death under the Law of Apostasy.

It has been argued that this kind of "protection" can ultimately change the very personality of an entire group of people. Parallels are sometimes made between the "dhimmi" consciousness with that of being a hostage. The context is one of vulnerability which annuls the notion of rights and condemns the dhimmi/hostage to exude gratitude for being tolerated.[13]

The four centuries up until 1918, when the Ottoman Empire held sway over the Middle East, saw the "dhimmi" status of Christians maintained through the "millet" (community) system. The growth of Arab nationalism in the later nineteenth century ushered in a new chapter in Christian-Muslim relations in as much as it stood for a shared identity and citizenship for all Arabs within independent nation states. With the exception of Lebanon, however, *"in numbers the old inferiorisation would persist and - predictably – in mood as well. It would do so in new and untried form, however ardent the Christian participation".*[14]

The way this aspect of the region's religious heritage resonates in each Middle Eastern country depends on its specific history, current political context and the vigour to which the international debate on human rights is carried on locally.

It was interesting to note in the course of the visit that the Orthodox were much more reticent than other Christians about talking of the negative aspects of "dhimmitude", the issue of how to relate to and support Muslims who have, despite the context, converted ("illegally") to Christianity, the implications, even possibilities, of mixed marriages etc.

Egypt and Lebanon are very different countries. The last Coptic prime minister in Egypt was assassinated in 1910.[15] The policy of the modern Egyptian Arab (not Islamic) Republic towards minority religions is to some extent influenced by its local Islamist political tendencies. Fundamentals such as the conversion issue are not officially questioned and the regulations concerning church buildings remain strict, providing a continuing bone of contention between Christians and the Government. As an alternative to building churches, the Coptic Orthodox community has developed a system of fraternities which, in a way, helps to ameliorate the situation.

13 See Bat Ye'or, "The decline of Eastern Christianity under Islam: from Jihad to Dhimmitude", Associated University Presses, 1996, pp. 221-240.
14 Cragg.p.26
15 Cragg pp.171 and 198

Lebanon, unlike Egypt, is a country where Christians see their future bound up with their official recognition as one of the constituent religious groupings in the country. At the highest level this finds expression in the political system where the president is a Maronite, the prime minister a Sunni Muslim and the speaker of parliament a Shi'a etc. Any developments that might upset the country's (religious) demographic balance between Christians and Sunni and Shi'a Muslims are therefore very sensitive. Lebanese church leaders still insist on an established Christian role in Lebanon as a way of preserving not only the Lebanese Church but also the church in the region. As Wael Kheir told us, *"If you abolish confessionalism in Lebanon you abolish civil society, which in turn undermines democracy".*

2.   Arabism and identity

The belief in the Middle East as "an Arab world" was not difficult to hear, particularly in Lebanon and Syria - a place for Arab Jews, Arab Christians and Arab Muslims living side by side – an expression of an inclusive *Ummah* or united household of Islam. The hope for an "Arab Middle East" does not, of course, sit well with the non-Arab minorities in the region, as we heard clearly from Armenian Catholicos Aram.

The Copts, the major Christian presence in the region have long had a problematic relationship with Arabist Muslims. *"It would be fair to say,"* according to Kenneth Cragg, that *"there is something quite un-Arab about Coptic monasticism. To this day a strong instinct persists in Islam to see Coptic piety as an odd anachronism"*[16] The antiquity of "Egyptian-ness" has led the essence of Egypt often to be likened to a palimpset, a parchment on which the old survives beneath the new, as scribes in sequence write upon a fading past. *"Coptic Christianity is the text that persists below the Arabic and the Arabism of Islam and is itself a superscription on pharaonic Egypt through the Greco-Roman heritage."*[17] Reading such a script is nothing if not complex.

In the world view of an "Arab" Middle East under predominantly Muslim sway, Israel, understood as being a creation of Western Zionists, has no place. Its invasive presence, as Arabs perceive and feel it, is not simply another colonialism. Zionism is, for Zionists, essentially about reclaiming "the mother country" and is not therefore a colonialism ever minded to retreat.[18] It is not therefore difficult to understand the Arabist logic of Ahmed the Hizbollah fighter who would drive Israel into the sea. Such a stance is an extreme version of a deep anxiety about the

16 Cragg, p.176
17 Cragg, p.172
18 Cragg, p.27

90

Zionist presence that is felt within Christian as well as Muslim circles. At the political level, however, in the official stance of the PLO and the leadership of Egypt, Jordan and Syria, if not Iraq, the existence of Israel is no longer seriously questioned, for reasons of *realpolitik* if not conviction. Its nature, however, is another matter. As Patriarch Hazim crisply put his vision of the Middle East - *"not without Judaism too - though not Zionism".*

Christian identity is, in such an environment, exquisitely complex and challenging. The dominant religious force seeks to impose a political theology based on a "revealed certainty" which is only truly accessible in the Koran, i.e. through the medium of Arabic. The Christian scriptures, as translated into Arabic, are difficult for the Koranic-trained mind to enter into, even if the theological barrier of the Trinity is not an insuperable obstacle to the "good Muslim". The nature, origins and stories of the New Testament declare the Greek as well as Semitic roots of Christianity and render its Middle Eastern followers susceptible to pressure by those who would question their Arabist credentials.[19] In order to develop the inter-Arab encounter between Christian and Muslim, a question put by a leading Maronite layman echoes from our visit. It was left hanging in the air in Beirut, but it seemed very apposite - *"Perhaps we need to look again at what we understand by 'Arab'?"*

3.   Christian influence

In most of the countries we visited Christians at one time exercised much more political, economic and cultural influence than they do now. There used, of course, to be many more of them. Furthermore, they took most of the opportunities which opened up to them once the restrictions of the Ottoman period were lifted. A Christian "political dynamic" was, indeed, at work in the development of the Arab nationalist movement which emphasized equality for Muslims and Christians.

Educationally and in terms of health care the Christian population has made a disproportionate contribution to the building of civil society and its infrastructure. This is true throughout the region, and was something we witnessed directly in Egypt, Palestine and Lebanon. The reduction of the Christian population due to the changing political and religious situation in the region has naturally had the impact of reducing the Christian contribution.

In Egypt the nationalisation of the economy under Nasser impacted most particularly on the (expatriate) Greek and Armenian communities, although it

---

19 Cragg, p.282

affected the economic base upon which Coptic charitable work was done and on the security of Coptic monasticism.

In post-war Lebanon adjustments to the political system have been made to accommodate the growing Shi'a community, a development in which Syria's hand can be seen. The Maronite Church exercises great influence. It was around Maronite aspirations that the Lebanese identity and state were essentially created and it remains, in some ways, the predominant voice among Lebanese Christians.

In Syria Christians were particularly influential in the creation of the Arab National movement. The Ba'ath Party was founded jointly by a Muslim and Christian (Michel Aflaq). Though Christian "technocrats" can achieve high administrative office, Christians have never been close to real political power.

Similarly in Jordan, Christians are essentially excluded from real politics. They retain a major role in the economy, channelling their energies into other such areas of influence.

Throughout the region, Islam holds the upper hand in national constitutions that prohibit conversion and in Shari'a law being seen as a principal source for civil law. As has already been noted, Islam has always put parameters on religious freedom. With the growth of the Islamist movement there are now profound pressures on Islamised society and the relationship between Islamic law and the "public space" is a natural arena of change and debate. How far Christians participate in such a process will be indicative of the influence they feel able to seek.

4.   Christian confidence

In the course of the visit a range of socio-religious factors was noted which contributed to undermine Christians' confidence.

Egypt has witnessed a profound but gradual Islamisation of society since the 1970s. Though in the course of our visit there were none of the occasional, and generally disapproved, eruptions of anti-Christian violence, the feeling of Christian professionals there was that their prospects for advancement in employment are quietly restricted by a distinctly thick "glass ceiling". (Indeed, it may be recalled that, at the national political level, Boutros Boutros Ghali, before his period at the UN, was the effective Foreign Minister of Egypt, but was always known as Deputy Foreign Minister!)

Occasionally violence breaks out between government forces and Islamists. It would be difficult and possibly unacceptable if a Christian officer led an operation against Muslims. This would give support to the claim that the government is "non-Islamic" and allows Christians to bear arms. This would be against the Dhimma status and would not be well received within majority Muslim opinion.

In southern Lebanon the church leadership reports young Christians as feeling they have "lost out" – against the constitutionally necessary rise in Muslim influence following from the Taif Agreement which ended the civil war. It must be remembered that the Lebanese-Israeli conflict started over the presence of Palestinian militants in the area. Palestinian-Christian Lebanese conflict started at this point. Hence the general, but not universal, support among southern Lebanese Christians for Israel. The removal of the Israelis from the so-called 'southern security zone' has also undermined their presence.

There is a sense of being neglected by a Lebanese Government which is not acting particularly quickly to re-establish its authority in the south, preferring, probably at Syria's behest, to let Hizbollah maintain its presence, if only *"to keep Israel on its toes"*, as Prime Minister Hariri put it. This echoes the important relationship between Syria and Iran, which we saw epitomised by Ahmed at al-Khiam.

In Syria and Jordan, inter-religious relations were noticeably cordial on the surface but constrained by the politico-theological reality of Islam beneath it. In Syria, largely Sunni in Muslim terms, that reality involves the control of the ruling Ba'ath Party by the minority Alawites.

All the recognized churches within the Syrian Christian community benefit to some degree financially from the State, yet it is only the Orthodox who are seen truly as part of the "fabric of society". Even the Catholics are still seen by some as outsiders to some extent. It was, in fact, as long ago as the sixteenth century that the Greek Catholic community emerged from the ranks of the Orthodox Patriarchates. It is now virtually the most Arab of all the churches.

Within Israel Christians have long played a leading role in local politics, particularly where the Christian population is strongest. At the national level Azmi Bishara, a Christian from Haifa, stood as a candidate for Prime Minister in 1999.

In recent times, as Arab Israelis have responded in more active ways to the Israeli-Palestinian crisis, a new edge has entered even long-standing personal relationships between Christians and Muslims. Whereas not so long ago religious identity was, for many, hardly an issue in the course of everyday relationships, now the situation is different - though it is not an issue susceptible to easy generalization.

Experiences over the last two years in Nazareth - over the proposed mosque next to the Latin Basilica and Muslim violence against Nazareth Christians as they left Easter Vigil services in 1999 - have been significant. Christians who have long understood they are a double minority, Arabs in a Jewish State and Christians in a largely Muslim Arab population, may be excused worrying about what the future may hold should fundamentalist Muslims and right-wing Israelis choose, if only for temporary, opportunistic reasons, to join forces. This is not a far-fetched possibility. The Christian-Muslim tension in Nazareth came to a head after meddling by right-wing Israeli politicians looking for Muslim votes in the Israeli elections. More worrying still, there were reports from very credible sources of collusion between the Islamist activists and Israeli intelligence and security forces.

In Palestine many Arab Christians appear to have internalised the attitude of a religious minority, and tend to leave political life to others. On the West Bank and in Gaza, the role of Christians in politics is largely dependent on selection for appointive or consultative office. Apart from Hanan Ashrawi, the only Christians elected to the Palestinian legislative assembly were chosen for seats guaranteed to Christians from Bethlehem, Jerusalem and Ramallah.[20] As the Jerusalem church leaders advised us, there is no black-and-white picture.

5.   Emigration

There is no doubt that there is anxiety about the future of Christianity in the Middle East. Emigration is generally increasing and the rate of Christian emigration is greater than average – at least in Lebanon, Jordan and, most precipitously, in Palestine. The reasons for this enduring phenomenon are various. Nineteenth century Christian mission invested in education, a tradition maintained by Christian churches today to some extent. Trained and qualified people have more options to exercise than most. They include Muslims educated at Christian schools, but the Muslim population can more easily bear the loss. However, where conflict rages, or post-conflict balances change, decisions take on a very serious, even urgent quality, especially in the Palestinian Christian Triangle in the West Bank (Bethlehem-Beit Jala-Beit Sehour). There is a real danger to the long-term survival of the "living stones", even within a generation.

---

20 Fr. Drew Christiansen, "Christian participation in Islamic societies", First Congress of Patriarchs and Bishops of the Middle East, May 1999, Harissa, Lebanon.
Available on http://www.al-bushra.org/mos-chr/christian.htm

6. Christian mission

Wherever we went the indigenous MECC member churches emphasized the Islamic reality within which they live and, to them, the correctness of conceiving of Christian mission in their context as Christian service. At its best such an approach brought to life an incarnational theology that in some places sustained an almost joyful willingness to suffer - alongside a commitment to empower the powerless of whatever religious culture. Personal redemption was not the key issue. This was most clearly seen in Orthodox contexts.

This approach was in some state of tension with that of some New (Protestant) Churches which, drawing from their western mission-based history, have a commitment to personal evangelism - even among the indigenous Christian minority. Perhaps it is not entirely surprising that they experience at the level of church leadership or formal inter-church relations a sense of marginalisation! On the other hand their own tendency to cling on to Western cultural forms of expression, not seriously attempting the contextualisation of theology, worship, liturgy and music alienates them from Eastern fellow Christians and non Christians alike.[21]

The particularities of mission differ between Orthodox, Catholics and Protestants and the strongly "evangelical/charismatic" community. These differences are not understood by the "Muslim street". All Christian mission is taken as a reminder of the Crusades, if not as evidence of a modern crusade. For their collective advantage, Christians need more unity in action.

7. The task of dialogue

Catholicos Aram reminded his CTBI visitors of the need to pursue a "dialogue of life", facing the daily realities of a plural society in the Lebanon. The difficulties of achieving this were evident in our time in that recovering country, despite hearing that it would not be long before Lebanon would show its beautiful, broadly "ecumenical" face to the world again as an inspiration to others.

At an inter-church level the need for dialogue remains an essential ecumenical task. Relations between the Orthodox and the Evangelical family, for example, need to be understood by differentiating the ecumenically-minded churches that are the products of mainline western missions, from the anti-ecumenical "evangelicals" which are accused of practising proselytism in the most derogatory sense of that word. Evidence of the "theologico-political" tension with some aggressive,

---

21 Revd Dr Habib Badr, "The Protestant Evangelical Community in the Middle East", International Review of Mission, Vol. LXXXIX, No.352. p.65

western, pro-Zionist evangelical churches is not limited to Jordan, though that is where the CTBI group most clearly encountered it.

While such dialogue must be pursued and deepened, fundamental theological difficulties between Christianity and Islam also need to be recognized for what they are. After all, both faiths appeal to a "sacred book" as central to their tradition. Some of the stories even overlap, though their interpretation is not identical. Both claim to be "revealed", and on this there is a real division between the Christian and the Muslim. Given this reality, Patriarch Hazim said, *"look at me!"* meaning that dialogue should be based on the interaction of persons, not the thrashing out of texts. This is what many a Christian would say and, plausibly, perhaps even Grand Mufti Khuftaro.

From the perspective of Islam, of course, Christian disunity proves its error. That is why Muslim history suggests Islam emerged. The continuing "witness" of ecclesiastical disunity is not a challenge to Islam, but a confirmation of its rightness and succession to Christianity. Fragmentation weakens the bonds of Christianity in the region, which in turn leads to loss of identity and confidence and then emigration. This suggests a need for serious theological engagement with the question of Christian disunity, Christian "mission and evangelism" towards other churches and how this plays to the Islamic environment and Muslims' self-identity – even among British and Irish Christians who take disunity as a given and possibly do not see the connection between Christian ecumenism and inter-religious dialogue in the region.

8.   Ecumenical responses

At the 1999 Assembly of the MECC the need for concern about "Christian Presence" to permeate the organization's work was agreed. It was not to be hived off into a special department. The Revd Dr Riad Jarjour, MECC General Secretary, has since characterized the Middle East as a region of 'anxiety and hope'. Addressing the question of Christian Presence he advocates a positive and purposive ecumenical approach.

"Strengthening Christian presence requires greater solidarity among the churches, their sustained effort to coordinate and work together in the areas of Christian ministry, social services, education, cultural activities and communications. Solidarity will encourage Christians in their common devotion to the gospel of Jesus Christ. It will strengthen their self-confidence, and be a factor in deepening their resolve to remain in their land. This cannot be achieved if Christians do not work together at a rapprochement which, respecting the diversity of tradition, does not quickly or lightly cast aside or ignore doctrinal differences but which, at the

same time, prevents making confessional peculiarities into obstacles that distanced Christians from each other and impede their coming together in one witness to Jesus Christ. "[22]

One of MECC's most important roles is to facilitate Christian reflection on its Islamic context in the Middle East and to further the cause of Christian-Muslim understanding. The MECC and the Arab Working Group on Christian-Muslim Relations organised a major dialogue event in Cyprus, 16-18 November 2000 which drew 40 participants from the Arab world and other countries where Christians and Muslims are in conflictive situations. Before them was a draft text produced by the Arab Working Group entitled *Dialogue and Co-existence: Toward an Arab Muslim-Christian Covenant.*

The process of discussing this important document goes on -in order that it may become part of the "dialogue of life" of which Catholicos Aram spoke.

---

22 See "Christian Presence in the Middle East: A Working Paper", MECC, in International Review of Mission, Vol. LXXXIX, No.352, p.31

Chapter 6

Perceptions of the West

1.   Within the Christian family

HH Pope Shenouda made a point of telling the CTBI group visiting Egypt how disconcerted he had been when Prince Charles declared his interest in conceiving his future role as "Defender of Faith". A sentiment which some in Britain had interpreted in positive "inter faith" terms at home led the leader of the largest Christian community in the Middle East to ask, "*where is Western support for Middle Eastern Christianity? Why don't Western Christians understand how their behaviour affects the churches in the Middle East?*"

Was Pope Shenouda merely reflecting in these questions a simple concern for "Christian Presence", or was he saying bluntly that Western Christians just do not see or recognize their Middle Eastern brothers and sisters, largely Arab by ethnicity, let alone understand their vulnerability within the sea of Islam? Or was he reflecting a particularly Coptic Orthodox perspective not unrelated to his own incarceration and exile by President Sadat?

The British churches are also seen themselves as complicit in false British political moves in the Middle East. This is a perception based more on ignorance than anything else. The Middle Eastern churches generally claim not to know of British churches' engagement with their government concerning Iraq throughout the 1990s. British churches are also presumed to support Israel over against the Palestinians, despite the growth of awareness of some of the latter as Christianity's "living stones".

2.   Politically – the UK

Unsolicited negative perceptions of the responsibility of the United Kingdom for some of the present suffering in the Middle East are easy to come by in the region, from Egyptian villages to Gaza slums and the seats of authority of prime ministers and patriarchs. Orthodox Christianity is but one local tradition in which memories are very long.

Within the Palestinians there is a strong memory of the way their community was dealt with at the hands of pro-Zionist British leaders (Lloyd George, Balfour, Churchill) in the thirty-odd years before their "Nakba" (Catastrophe) of 1948 and the failure of Britain to resist American pro-Zionist pressure after the Second

World War.[23] Britain is thus expected to play a major part in undoing the damage which it helped to inflict on the Middle East by appearing to promise the same piece of land to two different peoples, one of which had long been in occupation.

Questions constantly arise: why is it that Britain follows the USA so slavishly, apparently, and is unconcerned with the "double standards" of which it is regularly accused. It is not just a matter of drawing the issues of Israel-Palestine and Iraq uncomfortably together - where were Britain and its allies in responding to the invasion of Cyprus by Turkey and Lebanon by Israel? And is not Israel on the periphery of Europe - geopolitically not a thousand miles from the Balkans?[24]

These sentiments are not, of course, unknown within the Foreign and Commonwealth Office. The official response is normally couched in terms of recognizing the need for Britain to use its influence in the most appropriate manner, i.e. by quiet diplomacy which, by its very nature, works against a more open acknowledgement of the issues at stake. On the other hand, because quiet diplomacy can hardly be externally monitored, there is no knowing how much engagement there has been with the parties at any one time or, in much detail, the terms.

There is also the question of 'British interests' which form part of foreign policy, and which have for some time been pursued alongside an "'ethical dimension" which the Rt.Hon.Robin Cook MP, then Foreign Secretary, enunciated in 1997. The judgement as to when these two facets conflict may ultimately be the Prime Minister's. In the recent past, the Department of Trade and Industry's naming of Israel as a "market target", a development which has been welcomed by the Israeli business community, has not been seen as inconsistent with the EU's closer scrutiny on technical grounds of the human rights provisions in the EU-Israel Trade Association Agreement.

---

[23] See the Revd Dr Donald Wagner "Dying in the Land of Promise", Melisende 2001, especially chapter 5 (The ambivalence of hand and voice: Palestine under Britain 1920-1948)

[24] On 22 April 1999, at the height of the Kosovo crisis, the Rt Hon Tony Blair, Prime Minister, made an important speech in Chicago entitled "Doctrine of the International Community". Accepting that 'non-interference' has long been considered an important principle of international order, he argued against jettisoning it too readily. But he said that it should now, in a rapidly globalizing world, be qualified in some respects…..in cases of genocide and "when oppression produces massive flows of refugees which unsettle neighbouring countries". These situations he described as "threats to international peace and security". The Palestinians could be forgiven for believing that this essentially describes a significant part of their reality and wonder why there is, in their experience, no commensurate decisive international support, notwithstanding EU financing of the PA and UNRWA budgets.

3.   Politically – Ireland

Ireland's commitment to the United Nations and, in particular, to providing practical peace-keeping support operations has long been recognized. Indeed the Irish served in this capacity in the Lebanon all through the period of Israeli occupation.

At various points in the CTBI journey local awareness of Ireland's engagement in international affairs was evident and appreciation voiced. Ireland's lack of "political baggage" compared with Britain was recognized and hopes expressed that Ireland could make the most of that within those EU forums which consider policy on the Middle East, particularly Israel-Palestine. After the delegation returned it was noticeable that the Irish Government felt able to "go public" in much more explicit terms than the British in the response to the Mitchell Committee's report [25] The first major public British expression of concern about the Israel-Palestinian crisis for some time was not made until 10 July when the Rt Hon Jack Straw, the new Foreign Secretary issued a statement expressing his concern over the demolition of Palestinian houses in Jerusalem on 9 July and during the following night in Rafah, Gaza. He said: "I call on the Government of Israel to ensure that no more demolitions take place. I urge all parties to act with restraint, and indeed look for ways of building trust, in the spirit of the Mitchell Report."

---

25 The evidence for this is the substantial Statement made in the Senate by Mr Brian Cowen TD, the Minister for Foreign Affairs, on 24 May.

Chapter 7

Jerusalem Reflections

1.   Preliminary Reflections

The following 16 points constituted part of a Press Release prepared at the end of the visit before the CTBI delegation left Jerusalem.

1.   The Intifada began among deprived Palestinians in despair at the failure of the seven-year "Oslo Peace Process" to deliver either peace or prospects of prosperity. The weight of the Israeli response has subsequently created a situation of indescribable suffering among Palestinians within the Occupied Territories and deep anxiety and uncertainty throughout the Middle East, which is in danger of fanning the flames of extremism.

2.   Violence, whether from stick or stone, or lethally from tank and helicopter-gunship, has not and will not solve the Palestine-Israel crisis; nor will simplistic calls from the Israeli Government to Yasser Arafat to "stop the violence".

3.   The Israeli claim to have acted with restraint in response to the Intifada does not bear examination. A senior Israeli Government official told the delegation that "if there is one building standing in Beit Jala after they fired at Jerusalem, it means that we have not responded at all…if there are more Palestinians dead it is because we shoot better."

4.   Given the asymmetries of power between Israel and the Palestinians, it is incumbent on the Israeli Government not to act with grossly disproportionate force.

5.   Deep questions of the meaning of "non-racism" and "security" face Israeli society in the wake of 33 years' illegal occupation which were summed up by one Palestinian saying, "Everything conspires to tell us that we don't count. In the name of security they get away with murder".

6.   The generally accepted "two-state" solution to satisfy competing claims between Israelis and Palestinians must allow independence to both states and must also be implemented in a way which recognizes the need for interdependence between the two nations. The devastation of Palestinian lives- economically,

financially, socially and culturally - by repeated "closures" will not provide the trust upon which such a relationship could develop.

7.   Questions of identity, whether of Arab, Jew, Israeli, Palestinian, Christian or Muslim, need to be respected within frameworks of peaceful cooperation and co-existence.

8.   The crucial issue of a "Right to Return" for refugees is one marked by conflicting perceptions. From Israelis we heard of the need to preserve the integrity of the Jewish State. From Palestinians we heard of the need to recognize not only a past injustice but a present right, even though that right may not be capable of being fully exercised.

9.   The acute human need resulting from the severe political, economic and social problems of the last six months in Israel-Palestine urgently require more international aid from both governments and non-governmental organizations.

10.   In the region which is the cradle of the three great Abrahamic faiths - Judaism, Christianity and Islam - religion is not itself a cause of conflict, and in many instances is a source of reconciliation. A pluralistically-minded Zionist Jew told the delegation that "the land does not belong to us - we belong to the land - and the same can be said of Christians and Muslims". The same speaker also averred that "there can be no peace without truth and reconciliation".

11.   Inter faith contact and dialogue in the Middle East (as also in Britain and Ireland) must assume ever higher priority in a shrinking world.

12.   The Palestinian struggle for independence will not cease, partly because of the strengths within Palestinian civil society which compensate for some of the failings of the Palestinian Authority.

13.   The concern of the early Christian communities for the church in Jerusalem needs today to be translated into an active support of the churches throughout the Middle East. Churches are fast declining in numbers because of the intense pressure of violence, injustice and emigration. Additionally, they feel invisible to and neglected by their fellow Christians in the West.

14.   The Churches of the West need to recognize and try to help reverse the drastic reduction in pilgrimages which, in recent months, has had catastrophic consequences in Jerusalem, Bethlehem, Nazareth and other places.

15.   The British and American Governments, in particular, need to re-examine their Middle East policies so as to support the emergence of solutions to the region's problems that primarily serve the best interests of the people who live there. All over the region the cry of "double standards" is loudly heard, contrasting Western policy on Israel with that on Iraq and other countries which defy UN Resolutions.

16.   The British Government and people need to recognize their particular contribution to the history of the region and hence responsibility for some of its problems. There is a belief that Britain, with its European partners, could and should play a stronger political and economic role so that it be no longer said that Britain betrayed its Mandate and has since failed to live up to its responsibilities.

(A perspective very similar to that given by CTBI on 24 March was articulated in the USA on 20 April by Richard Falk,[26] Professor of International Relations at Princeton University. On the basis of visiting Israel and the Occupied Territories on a UN mission in February, three weeks before CTBI, he has gone on record as saying that, 'The circumstances of the Palestinians are worse than my moral imagination is capable of depicting. The present modalities of Israeli occupation impose on every Palestinian a daily ordeal, whether closures, checkpoints, incursions, or random attacks. Israel's larger design includes a desire to break the will of Palestinians to resist and to fasten a permanent structure of dominance onto the territories. The Israeli public, with some notable exceptions, lacks any real understanding of the Palestinians' daily suffering.")

2.   Reflections revisited

The 16 points which make up the substance of the CTBI Press Release of 24 March 2001 can bear scrutiny in the light of the period which has elapsed since the visit.

The downward spiral of the Israeli-Palestinian relationship only validates the judgements made in points 1 to 6. The tragic developments in April and May, including the hugely misjudged use of F16s by the Israeli Government and the Tel Aviv suicide bombing which claimed 20 young Israeli lives only adds a sense of urgency to the need for a just peace and lasting solution to be found – for the sake of all the peoples of the Middle East. Ten years ago Irish churches were involved in an "ecumenical trialogue" with counterparts from South Africa and the Middle

---

[26] Richard Falk was speaking at the Center for Policy Analyis on Palestine Washington in a symposium entitled "The Israel-Palestine Predicament: How to end an Occupation"

East. Perhaps the Irish search for peace and justice since then (still, of course, "work in progress") is a resource that should be further explored.

In point 7 the critical issue of identity which lies at the heart of the difficulties in many Middle Eastern relationships is noted. This point has regional, political and religious connotations. Its addressing is part of the essential agenda of the MECC, which has the unique responsibility of fostering ecumenical connections and mutual learning throughout the region – in the Arab-Christian Working Group and its programmes on Human Rights, Church Life, Gender and Development.

Point 8 implies the need for recognition of past wrongs by Israel, and the willingness of a sovereign Palestine to negotiate so as to remove from the Israeli psyche the idea that there is no end to Palestinian demands and to enable Palestinian refugees to build the new futures that have for so long been denied them – in the new Palestine, within Israel and in third countries.

Point 9 is self-explanatory but its implementation is to some extent contingent on circumstances on the ground.

From Points 10 and 11 several things follow:
- a commitment to strengthening the contribution of the Christian Presence in the Middle East so that the reconciling vision of the Christian message not be lost, squeezed between the completing claims of Jews and Muslims;
- the encouragement and strengthening of inter faith "justice, peace and reconciliation" work within Israel and between Israelis and Palestinians;
- clarification of how Middle Eastern Christians can unite in the struggle for peace and justice in the Holy Land;
- clarification of the role of Middle Eastern Christians on the periphery of Israel-Palestine can play within their own societies and in relation to the Israel-Palestine crisis;
- consideration of the timeliness, even necessity, of new efforts being made within Britain and Ireland to promote inter faith understanding and witness for justice over Israel-Palestine.

Point 12 may become even more critical should the Palestinian Authority founder under Israeli financial, political and, indeed, physical pressure. The relationship of Palestinian NGOs with the PA has never been particularly harmonious, a phenomenon not unknown in other "liberation" contexts, but its disappearance would put the PNGO constituency under a new kind of exposure to Israeli power.

The commitment of the PNGOs to participatory development also has longer-term implications for the strengthening of civil society elsewhere in the region.

Points 13 and 14 would be of specifically direct concern to the churches of CTBI. Reference should be made to the recommendations of the 1981 and 1990 visits and questions asked of where progress has been made and where more could be done.

Points 15 and 16 relate to the particular stances of the UK, EU and USA and require sustained ecumenical work in order adequately to be addressed.

There is no doubt that the UK, EU and USA are highly concerned with recent developments in the region. Strong messages have been given in public and in private to the contending parties. The proposals contained in the Mitchell Report, in which the EU had a hand, are strongly backed as a package of measures which, if implemented in the phased, confidence-building, way could enable peacemaking to stage a recovery.

The USA is acknowledged on all sides to be a critical external actor. The Republican Bush Administration has given rather conflicting signals about its agenda in the region. Despite an early "hands-off" attitude, it has more recently expressed support for some form of international observer presence and, therefore, may be preparing the ground for a more serious re-engagement. Behind the Administration, however, is an American public which has largely been led to believe, by American politicians and media, as well as advocates for the Israeli Government, that Yasser Arafat bore sole responsibility for the collapse of the Camp David talks in August 2000. This is, in actual fact, a travesty of the truth.[27] There is little doubt that American perceptions - in the public domain as well as in the corridors of power - will continue to play a significant role as the Israel-Palestine crisis unfolds. Their interplay will influence whether and in what manner the USA engages.

---

27 Blaming Arafat for the failure of the peace process is a dangerous mistake. See "Camp David: a tragedy of errors" by Robert Malley (adviser to President Clinton on Arab Israeli affairs) and Hussein Agha (Oxford University) *The Guardian* 20 July 2001.

Chapter 8

Matters arising for the British and Irish churches

Text for preliminary meditation:
"Delegations come, delegations go, nothing ever changes."
(Metropolitan Cornelius, Jerusalem)

1.   Introduction

In drawing up a list of "matters arising" there is a tension between the diversity of contexts within the Middle East which the visit encountered and the need, particularly given resources available, for British and Irish churches to focus on priorities that are both challenging and feasible. There is also the question of trying to ensure that the outcomes of the visit are not totally related to the Israel-Palestine crisis, even though it is true to say that its resolution is the key to a new chapter for all in the Middle East that is more just and hopeful.

In the paragraphs which follow the Israel-Palestine crisis figures in greater detail than any other dimension to the visit. In sections 5,6 and 9, however, wider Middle East relationship issues are consciously addressed.

2.   Evaluating past commitments

From experiences of the two previous ecumenical visits, in 1981 and 1989, many suggestions came forth encouraging British and Irish churches to engage more fully with the political, cultural and religious dimensions of the Middle East (see chapter 3)

In 1999 an initial CTBI survey of how member churches were understanding and responding to the Middle East Peace Process was made, which produced some information which demonstrated how some churches had "moved on" from the 1980s. The CTBI visit should provide the spur to deepen the churches' awareness of how they have been and are engaging with a peace process now in crisis. Some of the questions can be highlighted with respect to different levels of church life:

- Church leadership:
  How many times and in what terms have church leaders addressed themselves to questions of justice and peace in the Middle East? How challenged and/or constrained do church leaders feel when responding to calls for signs of solidarity from counterparts in the Holy Land?

How significant is the future of Christianity in the Middle East for churches which have no close organizational ties with the region? How can the experience of the Ecumenical Visit to the Middle East be shared at church leader level?

- National assembly/synod/bishops' meeting:
  How many times and in what terms have these bodies addressed themselves to questions of justice and peace in the Middle East? What are the primary issues which have had to be dealt with in these processes (e.g. Christian Zionism, Christian-Muslim relations, oil, sanctions) How far have tangible forms of solidarity with the "Living Stones" been developed? In what ways is the issue of practical support for struggling minority Middle Eastern churches being addressed?

- Regional diocesan/synod/provincial meeting:
  As for national level above.

- Local church
  What provision is being made for encouraging regular prayer for the Middle East? How can a "critical mass of Christians concerned for Middle East Peace" be generated? What are the successes of mobilization efforts to date? Where are the frustrations and limitations? How can they be overcome?

CTBI is encouraged to consider the format through which such questions can most usefully be addressed, more to aid planning for the future than in a purely retrospective spirit.

3. Revisiting the Principles

The 1996 Principles, (chapter 3) based on an internationalist vision, remain essentially valid though, in the aftermath of the Oslo Peace Process they require updating. The following reworking is offered for the consideration of CTBI member bodies and the Middle East Forum of the Churches' Commission on Mission .

The CTBI churches are asked to (re-)commit themselves to

Support the three-fold call of the Mitchell Report to both Israelis and Palestinians - end the violence, rebuild confidence, resume negotiations - and for the acceptance of its recommendations as a unified package by both sides.

Support the development of a new Peace Process in the wake of the failure of the Oslo Accords to deliver a final settlement, negotiated on the basis of UN Resolutions 181, 194, 242 and 338 which, *inter alia*, recognize the right of both communities, Palestinian and Israeli, to self-determination, security, international recognition and the protection of human rights (including the "right of return").

Endorse the call of Middle Eastern church partners for the Israeli Government to negotiate steps which will "End the Occupation", in the interests of security for Israel, peace for the Palestinians, and the transformation of relationships in the region.

Encourage sustained international commitment to rebuilding peace between the Israelis and Palestinians, and the achievement of an international agreement co-sponsored by parties acceptable to both sides.

Support British and Irish Government and European Union initiatives to encourage and facilitate the rebuilding of peace, the progress of which needs to include independent monitoring.

Encourage support by the British and Irish Governments, the EU and the wider international community for the Palestinian economy through, for example, investment in infrastructure, joint ventures and employment, and income-generating schemes.

Support for NGO and church-based initiatives focussed on encouraging the EU to hold both the Israeli Government and Palestinian Authority to account on human rights concerns in the course of negotiations on trade and development assistance.

Support the vision that Jerusalem is, in the words of Latin Patriarch Michel Sabbah, *"a city for two people and three faiths"*, i.e. a city of definitive importance for two national communities, the Israelis and the Palestinians, the status of which is defined by international law and long-standing agreements.

Monitor religious freedom within Israel-Palestine and press for the right of access to places of worship, and the right to gather for worship, issues which are vital for

Christians and Muslims resident in the West Bank who, because of the closures, are prevented from entering Jerusalem, and even for Muslim men under the age of 45 who are Jerusalemites.

Increase support for the Palestinian Christians and the churches of the Holy Land in their continuing presence and witness for peace with justice, through "alternative tourism", vigil prayer, financial and other practical support for church-based service institutions and joint advocacy.

Explore across religious boundaries the possibility of identifying new ways of witnessing for peace and justice in the interests of guaranteed security for Israelis and Palestinians.

Support for NGO and church-based thinking designed to keep the issue of "protection" for the Palestinians on the international agenda and to explore the potential role of internationally-recruited civil society peace observers.

4. Accepting the challenge of Middle Eastern church partners

Politically speaking this means endorsing the call to the Israeli Government to indicate that it will, without prejudicing other international obligations, take steps to "End the Occupation". This call needs to be understood in the following terms:

- It is a people's right to struggle against Occupation (which is illegal in international law).

- The Jerusalem Church Leaders believe and have testified that non-violent means are "stronger and more efficient" than violence. (Latin Catholic Patriarch Sabbah himself says that terrorism is *"illogical, irrational, and unacceptable as a means to resolve conflict".)*

However, again in Patriarch Sabbah's words,

- *"Violence has a cause, and the cause has to be removed in order to remove violence".* That cause is the Israeli military occupation of Palestinian land.

Therefore

- The rhetorical demand of the Israeli Government to Yasser Arafat "to end violence" is inadequate if not misconceived. Willing the end requires willing the means.

This is thus the critical step down the path which can and, indeed, must lead to security for Israel and peace for the Palestinians. It has the potential, if not the guarantee, of transforming relationships in the region.

The Church of Scotland, at its May 2001 Assembly, approved a Deliverance in which it "recognize(s) the fundamental difficulty represented by the fact of occupation or illegal annexation of territory by Israel, and reaffirm(s) that the withdrawal from such occupation is the first step towards a just and peaceful resolution of the conflict."

Each CTBI member body is asked to consider how it might address this issue in the interests of enabling the mind of the Churches Together to be discerned. This is a process which could also take place as a way of identifying with any broader movement that may emerge to promote the end of occupation.

(Although the parallels with apartheid South Africa are by no means exact, it is not untimely to recall that in 1989 the BCC, with the support of the Anti-Apartheid Movement, sponsored a significant conference on British policy towards Southern Africa. This led to the creation of the 100-member Southern Africa Coalition).

5.   Engagement with the international actors

The Israel-Palestinian problem has become a much more international crisis since the Israeli's lethal response to the stone-throwing that followed Ariel Sharon's visit to the Noble Sanctuary/Temple Mount in September 2000.

Monitoring the engagement of the main international players – USA, EU, UN, Arab League, Russia – requires specialized knowledge and organizational capacity. In ecumenical terms this is more easily found within a body such as Christian Aid than the great majority of CTBI churches, though there are a few which are experienced and committed to provide specific "added value". The international experience and potential coordinating role of the World Council of Churches also needs to be recognized.

Participating in the promotion of the desirable synergy between agencies and churches suggests **a continuing ecumenical role for CTBI**. The primary focus would naturally be the British and Irish Governments within the EU context, as a response to the challenge given to the CTBI delegation in many places that ecumenical efforts be made to encourage an EU stance more independent from that of the USA, and as constructive a role from the UK as from Ireland.

6.   Learning from the Middle East

The CTBI visit threw up possibilities of identifying new ways of engaging with Middle Eastern Christianity in its largely Muslim context. Given the nature of the relationship between Britain and the Middle East, the difficulty that the Middle East churches have had in hearing the British churches, the intentional exploration of such possibilities is timely if not overdue. The primary instrument of such an engagement would be the Churches' Commission on Mission (CCOM) Middle East Forum.

The delegation suggests that the Middle East Forum explores the idea that Syria and the Syrian churches be a special focus of ecumenical interest, attention, visitation and exchange over the next few years. The rationale can be couched in terms of a changing internal political environment, Syria's key role in Middle East peace-making and an interest expressed by Syrian Christians during and after the CTBI visit, particularly at the level of youth.

7.   Inter faith initiative?

Israel is, psychologically, a much-changed country compared with its pre-Camp David days. The election of Ariel Sharon indicated the shock that had been sustained to the national Israeli political psyche following the breakdown at Camp David talks (which the Palestinians felt were premature) and the outbreak of the Al-Aqsa Intifada. The nature of the Israeli response has caused heart-searching within some Jewish diaspora circles. If ever there was a time for a broadly ecumenical/inter faith commitment to human rights in the Middle East to be made manifest, now could be the time. It is a complex area, without doubt, but the questions of how and when such an initiative might be taken are more valid than why or why not.

CTBIís relevant staff are encouraged to consider whether this judgement is correct and, if so, to explore its practical implications.

8.   Decade to Overcome Violence

CTBI is encouraged to identify the cause of peace and justice in the Middle East as a key element in the British and Irish churches' response to the Ecumenical Decade to Overcome Violence. This could mean, inter alia, inviting representation of Middle Eastern churches at major ecumenical gatherings and facilitating their access to networks concerned with political, inter faith and mission concerns.

9.   Maintaining effective ecumenical relationships

It became clear at a number of points during the visit that there was a grave lack of awareness among Middle Eastern Christians of any of the official representations made by Churches in Britain and Ireland in support of human rights, justice and peace in the Middle East. Even if this is not wholly surprising, the question remains about how ecumenical communications with the Middle East can be made more effective.

For a discussion of the issues to be productive some aspects of current ways of working within churches, mission and development agencies might need to be reviewed. Some of the questions which could be addressed are:

- In what ways, if any, does current practice through which Middle East Forum member bodies relate to the Middle East foster **ecumenical communication?**

- What possibilities exist for denominational bodies (churches or agencies) which relate to the Middle East to broaden their horizons to include the making of relationships with ecumenical bodies such as MECC and to share their experience?

- In what ways can Christian Aid's partnership with the MECC facilitate the strengthening of broader ecumenical communications between British and Irish churches and Middle Eastern Christianity?

- What can CTBI itself do better to help Middle East Forum members and the Middle Eastern churches to hear one another more clearly?

Responding to the communications challenge of the Ecumenical Visit to the Middle East is, in some senses, **a responsibility of the entire membership of the CTBI and CCOM**. Coordination, primarily through the CTBI International Affairs and Communications Offices, and the CCOM Middle East Forum will clearly be essential.

Appendices

Appendix 1

Itineraries

Lebanon, 10–14 March

Participants:
Robert Davidson Christopher Gillham Esther Hookway Sigrid Marten Charles Reed Frank Turner Paul Renshaw John Waller

Saturday, 10 March

13.45	Depart London Heathrow T4
	Arrival Beirut Airport
	Met by MECC.
	Accommodation - Near East School of Theology, Hamra, Beirut.

Sunday, 11 March

08.00	Leave NEST for liberated South Lebanon, accompanied by Suad Hajj Nassif and Elie Azouz (MECC)
10.30	Arrival in Marjeyoun for latter part of Greek Orthodox service.
	Meeting with Bishop Kfouri at Greek Orthodox Bishopric.
	Lunch at Bishopric
	Visit Israel-Lebanon border fence near Fatima Gate - roof-top view of settlement for Russian immigrants to Israel.
	Visit MECC irrigation project.
	Visit Khiam prison
19.00	Return to Beirut.
20.00	Dinner with Dr Mary Mikhael (President, NEST), Revd Dr Victor Diab (Episcopal Church) and Mrs Diab, and the Revd Colin Chapman (Lecturer in Islamics, NEST).

Monday, 12 March

09:00	Sheikh Mohammad Rashid Kabbani, the Grand Mufti of Lebanon for the Sunni Community.
10:30	HH Catholicos Aram I, Armenian Apostolic Catholicosate of Cilicia
13.00	Sheikh Rafik El-Hariri, the Prime Minister of Lebanon. (CTBI delegation accompanied by Revd Dr Riad Jarjour, General Secretary, MECC)
14.30	Lunch
17.00	Ecumenical Forum (NEST) chaired by Dr Riad Jarjour
19.00	Reception at NEST

10.00   Bishop Elias Audi, Greek Orthodox Bishop of Beirut.
11.45   Kaslik University, Jounieh, with Fr Yousuf Mouanes (President of Kaslik University), Fr Elias Khalife (Associate General Secretary, MECC), Dr Wael Kheir and members of the Foundation for Human and Humanitarian Rights (Beirut).
             Leave for Beirut
13.00   Lunch with Bishop Boulos Matar (Maronite Bishop of Beirut) and Archbishop Kyrillos Bustros (Greek Catholic Archbishop of Baalbek)
14.30   Sabra-Shatila - Palestinian Refugees Camps - with Mrs Sylvia Haddad, Director of Joint Christian Committee for Social Work in Lebanon.
17.30   Return to NEST
18.00   Dr Mohammad Sammak, and Emir Hares Chehab (co-Chairmen) Christian-Muslim Dialogue Lebanese National Committee in Lebanon and other members of the committee, at NEST
20.30   Final Dinner at Al-Ajamy restaurant.

Programme of Sigrid Marten, Charles Reed and John Waller, 14-15 March:

15:        Excursion to Mount Lebanon (MECC work with displaced people) Foundation for Human and Humanitarian Rights
16:        Depart for Amman

Syria, 14-15 March

Participants:
Robert Davidson Christopher Gillham Esther Hookway Frank Turner

Wednesday, 14 March
08.00   Departure by road for Damascus
             Visit HB Raphael I Bidawid (Chaldean Patriarch of Babylon) before leaving Beirut.
14.00   Arrival in Damascus.
             Accommodation and lunch at Greek Orthodox Patriarchate
             Afternoon Free to visit Ummayid Mosque, Straight Street, Bazaar etc.
17.00   Mr Henry Hogger, British Ambassador, at the Residence
20.00   Dr Adnan Umran, Syrian Minister of Communications at his Ministry
22:00   Dinner with Mrs Mahat Farah El-Khoury of MECC and the Revd Stephen Griffith, the Archbishop of Canterbury's representative in Syria and Lebanon

Thursday, 15 March
09.10   HB Patriarch Ignatius IV Hazim (Greek Orthodox Church)
10.00   Revd Peter Zaour (Evangelical Church)
11.00   Grand Mufti Khuftaro at his house
12.30   Ananias House
13.00   Lunch

Afternoon Free
17.00   Bishop Isidore Batikha (Greek Catholic Church)
18.00   Greek Orthodox Lenten vespers
20.00   Ecumenical Forum (Holy Cross Halls, GOC): (Chaired by Mr Samer Laham, `
         Associate General Secretary, MECC) followed by light supper

Friday, 16 March
10.30   Abu Nour Mosque (Grand Mufti Khuftaro) - ecumenical homily on behalf of
         CTBI given by the Very Revd Dr Robert Davidson.
13.00   Lunch and departure by road for Amman
17.00   Arrive Amman

Egypt, 10-15 March

Participants:
Frederick George Gillian Kingston Michael Langrish Hywel Wyn Richards
Paul Renshaw (14-15 only)

Saturday 10 March
16.00   Departure from London Heathrow T4
         Arrival at Cairo Airport
         Met by Episcopal Diocese of Egypt
         Accommodation at Episcopal Guest House, Zamalek.

Sunday 11 March
10.30   Worship at All Saints Episcopal Cathedral
         Lunch at Guest House with Bishop Mouneer Anis and others
15.45   Departure by train for Beni Suef
17.45   Met by Sr Agapie Asaad, Daughters of Mary.
         Accommodation at Coptic Orthodox Centre, Bayad - Beni Suef
Evening "Christian life in an Islam-dominated society": discussion with Sr Agapie and five
         associated Coptic Brothers and Sisters.

Monday 12 March
09.00   Field Visit to Beni Suleiman Village with Coptic Evangelical Organization for
         Social Services (CEOSS)
11.30   Gathering at the Coptic Organization for Services and Training (COST)
12.00   Field Visit to Azhary Village with COST
16.30   Daughters of Mary Convent, Beni Suef
19.00   Return to Cairo by train

Tuesday 13 March
8.30   Mr Peter Gunning, Irish Ambassador to Egypt, at the Embassy.
Morning Visit Hod El Henna centres related to Coptic Orthodox Bishopric for Public,
         Ecumenical and Social Services (BLESS), arranged by Salwa Morcos.
AfternoonFree for visit to the Pyramids at Giza

20.15   HH Pope Shenouda III at St Mark's Cathedral, Abbassiya

Wednesday 14 March

09.00	Visit to the Egypt Museum
11.30	Revd Dr Safwat El-Baiadi, President of the Protestant Churches in Egypt, at Ramses College.
13.30	Arrival at Ramses College of Paul Renshaw (CTBI) from Beirut.
14.00	Lunch at Marriott Hotel
16.30	Bishop Youhanna Kolta, Deputy Patriarch, Coptic Catholic Church, Al Segoude Church, Soubra, with Mr Girgis Saleh, Associate General Secretary (MECC).
18.30	Midweek lecture by HH Pope Shenouda, St Mark's Cathedral, Abbassiya
21.00	Dinner with Bishop Mouneer and Mrs Anis.

Thursday 15 March

09.30	Kom Ghorab, Cairo with CEOSS (environmental project)
11.00	Churches of Coptic Cairo
13.00	Lunch and discussion at CEOSS headquarters, Heliopolis, with Nabil Abadir (Director) and senior staff.
15.00	Transfer to MECC headquarters for farewells
16.00	Leave for Cairo Airport.
19.45	Departure for Amman
21.15	Arrival at Amman Airport
	Met by Edmond Adam, MECC
	Accommodation at Grand Palace Hotel

Jordan, 16-17 March

Friday 16 March

09.00	Nahla Karmash Audeh and Edmond Adam (MECC staff) on ecumenical programmes in Jordan and MECC's involvement in Iraq, at MECC offices
11.00	Mr George Hazou, Chairman of the Near East Council of Churches Committee on Refugee Work, and other committee members.
12.00	Courtesy visit to local church leaders: Bishop Benedictus (Greek Orthodox), Archdeacon Salim (Episcopal Church)
13.00	Lunch at Al Bustan Restaurant
15.00	Ecumenical meeting with local clergy - Fr Ibrahim Dabbour (Greek Orthodox), Revd Samer Azar (Lutheran Church) and representatives of the Syrian Orthodox and Armenian Apostolic churches.
17.00	Rest and/or visit to Roman amphitheatre, old city of Amman.
18.30	Arrival of Beirut-Damascus Group
19.30	Dinner
	Accommodation at Grand Palace Hotel

<u>Saturday 17 March</u>
08.00   Departure by bus to Jordan-Israel border via Talbieh Refugee Camp (visit
         MECC-run centre), Madaba (visit old mosaic at St George's Church) and Mount
         Nebo (biblical site).
12.30   Pass through Jordanian passport control, cross bridge over Jordan river by transit
         bus and negotiate Israeli immigration formalities.
14.00   Rendezvous with bus sent from Jerusalem
         Proceed to Jerusalem
         Accommodation at Notre Dame Centre, adjacent to the Old City.

Israel-Palestine, 17-24 March

17.00   Welcome offered by Bishop Munib Younan, (Evangelical Lutheran Church),
         Chairman, International Christian Committee
         Initial briefing by Bishop Munib and Ramzi Zananiri, Executive Secretary, ICC.
         Dinner at Notre Dame

<u>Sunday, 18 March</u>
Morning Worship at the various Jerusalem Churches.
         Baptist Church   Fred George
         Church of the Redeemer   Gillian Kingston, Christopher Gillham
         Notre Dame   Frank Turner
         St Andrew's   Robert Davidson, Sigrid Marten, Paul Renshaw,
                                     Hywel Wyn Richards, John Waller
         St George's   Michael Langrish, Charles Reed
         St Jacob's   Esther Hookway
Afternoon Free - half of the party visited Yad Vashem
17.30   Reflection on experiences of Week One
18.30   Dinner at Notre Dame
Evening Further reflection on Week One

<u>Monday 19 March</u>
09.00   Tour the Old City of Jerusalem led by Hamil (Orient House)
13.00   Visit Haram Al-Sharif - Adnan Husseini, Administrator and sheikhs representing
         the Islamic Waqf
14.00   Lunch in Old City
15.30   "Perspectives for a post-Oslo Peace" - meeting and discussion with Dr Gershon
         Baskin and Dr Zakaria Al-Qaq (Israel-Palestine Centre for Research and
         Information.
17.00   free
18.30   Dinner at Notre Dame

<u>Tuesday 20 March</u>
09.00   Mr Avi Granot, Special Political Adviser to the President of Israel, at the Israeli
         Ministry of Foreign Affairs.
11.00   Dr Hanan Ashwari, Palestinian Legislative Council, at Orient House.

13.00	Lunch
15.00	Dr Thomas Neu (American Near East Refugee Aid) and Maha Aby Dayyeh. (Women's Centre for Legal Aid) representing International and Palestinian NGOs, at Notre Dame
17.00	Ecumenical meeting with church leaders, at Notre Dame:

Archbishop Paul Sayyah	Maronite Church
Archbishop Sewerios Malki Mourad	Syrian Orthodox Church
Metropolitan Timothy	Greek Orthodox Church
Bishop Aris Shirvanian	Armenian Apostolic Church
Fr Antonios Al-Urshalimi	Coptic Orthodox Church

18.30	Terry Greenblatt, Director, Bat Shalom (Daughters of Peace), at Notre Dame
20.00	Dinner at Papa Andrea's rooftop restaurant, Old City

Group visits:

Gaza   Michael Langrish, Sigrid Marten, Hywel Wyn Richards, Frank Turner

Wednesday 21 March

08.00	Depart Jerusalem: Arrive border crossing, met by MECC staff Mahmoud Okshiyya, Ibrahim Ghandour
09.45	Arrive Gaza City Visits to programmes of the Near East Council of Churches Committee for Refugee Works with Mahmoud Okshiyya, Ibrahim Ghandour and Costa Dabbagh (General Secretary) - Family Health Care Clinic, Mobile Dental Clinic, Young Men's Vocational Training
12.00	Mr Jabr M Wishah, Deputy Director, Palestinian Centre for Human Rights
13.15	Lunch, 'Al Salam' Restaurant, with the two from NECC-CRW and Munzer El Rayyes, Chairman of Agriculture Engineers' Association.
15.00	Field visit to agricultural areas under demolition attack from Israeli bulldozers etc, and visit to the orchard of Mr El Rayyes
18.00	Dr Haider Abdel Shafi, Chairman, Gaza Red Crescent Society and Commissioner General, Palestinian Independent Citizens' Rights Committee
19.00	Dr Ziad Abu-Amr, Chairman, Political Committee of Legislative Council
20.00	Dinner at 'Sea Breeze' Restaurant Overnight accommodation: Marna House

Thursday 22 March

09.00	Women's Activities and Young Women's Vocational Training (computers, dressmaking, etc, NECC-CRW)
10.15	Suhaila Tarazi, Director, Ahli Arab Hospital
11.45	Husam El-Nounou, Coordinator, Gaza Community Mental Health Programme
13.00	Lunch, 'Al Salam' Restaurant
14.30	Drive through refugee camp with Costa Dabbagh and colleagues, and depart Gaza
18.00	approx Arrival in Jerusalem

Galilee   Fred George, Christopher Gillham, Esther Hookway, John Waller

Wednesday 21 March
08.00   Depart Jerusalem
10.30   Arrive Nazareth: welcome by Judge Khalil Aboud, Chairman, ICC Galilee
11.00   Visit to Church of the Assumption (Greek Orthodox), Basilica of the
           Annunciation (Latin Catholic), old market.
12.30   White Mosque and meeting with the Custodian, Atef El Fahoum, followed by a
           late quick lunch.
15.30   Mayor of Nazareth
16.30   Fr Elias Chacour (Greek Catholic, founder of the Mar Elias educational
           institutions, Ibillin) Mr Fuad Haddad (Principal, Baptist School, Nazareth) and
           Revd Philip Saad (Chairman, Baptist Association of Israel) Hassan Jabbarin
           (Adalah, the Legal Centre for Arab Minority Human Rights) briefly, Mr Fuad
           Farah, Chairman of the Orthodox National Council, and Director of the Nazareth
           YMCA, Mohammed Zeidan (Arab Association of Human Rights)

Thursday, 22 March
10.00   Mr Nagib Rizik, former Deputy Mayor of Nazareth
           Two Greek Orthodox representatives
11.00   Bishop Boulos Marcuzzo (Latin Catholic)
12.00   Aida Suleiman (Women's Rights)
13.00   Lunch
           Visit to Nazareth Illit with Mohammed Zeidan
           Departure
19.30   Arrival in Jerusalem.

West Bank   Robert Davidson, Gillian Kingston, Charles Reed, Paul Renshaw

Wednesday 21 March
08.00   Depart Jerusalem
09.30   Arrive Hebron - link up with TIPH observer mission (Temporary International
           Presence in Hebron).
           Field visit to central Hebron – Jewish settlements.
11.30   Depart Hebron
12.30   Arrive Bethlehem. Visit Church of the Nativity
13.15   Lunch with Viola Raheb, i/c Lutheran schools in Palestine and Jordan.
14.30   Rev.Dr Mitri Raheb, Minister, Christmas Lutheran Church and Director of the
           International Lutheran Centre in Bethlehem.
15.15   Visit to Beit Jala and Aida camp, Bethlehem, escorted by Viola Raheb.
18.00   Dropped at checkpoint on Bethlehem-Jerusalem road; pick up sheroot to
           Jerusalem.

Thursday 22 March

09.15	Mr Robin Kealy (British Consul-General) plus counterparts from Sweden (Catharina Hempel Kipp), Ireland (Isolde Moylan) and the EU Commission (Jean Breteche) at the British Consulate-General, Sheikh Jarrah.
11.00	Canon Naim Ateek and Sabeel Board members (Jean Zaru, Cedar Duaybis, Samir Khoury) at Sabeel.
13.00	Lunch after midweek communion with Sabeel staff
16.00	Mr Azmi Bishara MK, at Notre Dame

Gaza and West Bank groups only

18.00	Bishop Riah Abu El-Assal, Episcopal Bishop of Jerusalem, at St George's.

CTBI group in toto

19.30	Rabbi Arik Aschermann, Yehezkel Landau, Debbie Weizmann (Jewish, associated with the Inter-Religious Coordinating Council of Israel), at Notre Dame.
21.00	Dinner at Notre Dame

Friday 23 March

09:30	Metropolitan Cornelius, Locum Tenens, Greek Orthodox Patriarchate.
10:30	HB Patriarch Torkum Manoogian, Armenian Apostolic Patriarchate.
12.00	Return to Notre Dame for initial consideration of Press Release.
	Lunch
15.30	Review and finalisation of Press Release
19:30	Farewell dinner at Nafoura Restaurant, Old City. Special Guests: Bishop and Mrs Munib Younan, Revd and Mrs Clarence Musgrave (St Andrew's)

Saturday 24 March

10.30	HB Patriarch Michel Sabbah, Latin Patriarchate
13.00	Departure for Tel Aviv Airport
16.55	Departure for London
20.10	Arrival at London Heathrow

Appendix 2

Jewish Chronicle (6 April 2001)
(Reprinted with permission)

Leading British Christians have returned from a two-week Middle East fact-finding mission denouncing Israeli actions in the occupied territories and declaring that the Palestinians are facing "indescribable suffering".

The 12-member delegation – which included an Anglican bishop and senior representatives for the UK's Roman Catholic, Methodist and Greek Orthodox communities – argued that Israel's response to the intifada was "fanning the flames of extremism".

In what Israeli and Jewish community officials criticised as a "distorted" overview, the delegation further suggested that Israeli claims to be acting with restraint "did not bear examination."

The clergy also reported that an unnamed Israeli official had told them during their visit that "if there are more Palestinians dead, it is because we shoot better."

The group added that "simplistic calls from the Israeli government to Yasir Arafat to stop the violence" were ineffectual.

Having visited under the auspices of the Churches Together in Britain group, the participant said in a preliminary report that they felt that it was "incumbent on the Israeli government not to act with grossly disproportionate force."

The Palestinian struggle for independence would not cease, they declared, "partly because of the strengths within Palestinian civil society, which compensates for some of the failings of the Palestinian Authority."

The churchmen also called on the British and American governments to reassess their Middle East policies. "All over the region the cry of 'double standards' is loudly heard, contrasting Western policy on Israel with that on Iraq and other countries which defy UN resolutions."

In his observations of the situation in Gaza, the Bishop of Exeter, the Right Revd Michael Langrish, noted: "The occupants of the (Jewish) settlements pay no taxes to the Palestinian Authority. There is water for their swimming pools, while many Palestinians are without adequate supplies for drinking and sanitation."

The Bishop went on to describe witnessing Israeli bulldozers destroying fields of crops in order to clear a road "for the use of a small number of settler families."

While welcoming the concern of the churches about the region, an Israeli embassy spokesman declared: "The notion that the story is simply about Palestinians being wronged by Israel is a gross distortion. And such a distortion does not serve the cause of peace."

The spokesman added that Ambassador Zvi Shtauber had this week enjoyed "cordial" meetings with the Archbishop of Canterbury, Dr George Carey, and the Archbishop of Westminster, Cardinal Cormac Murphy O'Connor. They spoke about the need for understanding and compassion when addressing the Middle East situation.

"The ambassador explained the importance of understanding the realities on the ground, rather than falling for the simplified image of one side being the aggressor and the other the victim."

Board of Deputies director-general Neville Nagler said the church leaders had failed to show understanding of the threats faced by Israelis, or take note of Palestinian leaders' "refusal to condemn and limit violence."

****

This article drew a response from one of the CTBI delegation, who was eminently qualified to pen it, on 27 April:

"Dear Sir,
May I respond briefly to the comments in your edition of the 6th of April concerning the recent visit of a delegation from the Churches Together in Britain and Ireland to the Middle East I was a member of that delegation. I also represent the Moderator of the General Assembly of the Church of Scotland as one of the Presidents of CCJ, and have spent my entire academic career encouraging Christian students to appreciate the Hebrew Bible. I have, therefore, every reason for encouraging "cordial" relationships between Jews and Christians, and have benefited greatly from my contacts with the Jewish community. Such contacts, however, do not mean that I am committed to looking at Israel uncritically.

There is indeed the "need for understanding and compassion when addressing the Middle East situation", the need to deplore violence from whatever source it comes. The Report, however, is concerned to "understand the realities on the ground", and it is these realities which lead to some of the comments in the preliminary report.

It is futile to call on Yasser Arafat to stop the present violence, or to insist on this as a rerequisite for further peace talks. Ariel Sharon's visit to the "Temple Mount" did not cause the present Intifada. It was but the spark which ignited long smouldering embers of Palestinian resentment and frustration, despair and a sense of humiliation, especially in the light of the failure of the Oslo Peace Process to deliver a meaningful future for the Palestinian people. The "realities on the ground" include the continued building and extension of settlements on the West Bank e.g. at Har Homa and Maale Adumim which make a Palestinian state more and more unrealistic. The story of what is happening in Israel/Palestine may not simply be about "Palestinians being wronged", but it is about the continuing relationship between the occupied and an occupation regime for Palestinians living within the pre-1967, UN guaranteed borders in the West Bank and Gaza. The psychological trauma and the daily economic hardships which this produces for Palestinians are seldom fully appreciated. You cannot stop violence unless you deal with the underlying reasons which make violence inevitable, and there is no evidence that Israel is prepared to do this.

If what happened to Palestinian houses in Beit Jala is compared with what has happened in Gilo, then it is hard to believe that Israel is acting with restraint, and it is equally difficult to find evidence for this in Hebron or Gaza. Few Israelis would now accept that Israel acted with restraint in the invasion of Lebanon in 1982, and there are Israelis today who are seriously concerned about what is happening now in their name on the ground.

Unless Israelis and Palestinians are treated as equal partners in the search for peace with justice, a peace which guarantees Palestinians freedom and hope, there will be no lasting security for Israel. It is because some of us care deeply about the future of Israel that we cannot keep silent about what is happening in Israel/Palestine. A Micah in Jerusalem today might have some harsh words to say about those who

> "covet fields and seize them;
> and houses and take them away:
> they oppress householder and house,
> people and their inheritance." (Micah 2.2)

Yours sincerely,

The Very Revd Professor Robert Davidson

Appendix 3

Middle Eastern Heads of Churches Meet, 20 November 2000

"Christianity in the East on the Threshold of the Third Millennium"

The leaders of 20 churches from around the Middle East, representing all four families of the Middle East Council of Churches, gathered at the Maronite Patriarchal seat in Bkirke for the third-ever meeting of the Heads of Churches in the Middle East.

The opening session was open to the public and the media. After worship led by HH Patriarch Zakka I Iwas of the Syriac Orthodox Church, four church leaders spoke, each on behalf of their church family. Their speeches were followed by the General Secretary's opening address.

HB Cardinal Patriarch Mar Nasrallah Boutros Sfeir, head of the Maronite Church, gave the first speech, on behalf of the Catholic family. He welcomed the assembled leaders to Bkirke, thanking them for honouring him with their presence. He followed with a brief history of the Catholic engagement with the ecumenical movement, and with the MECC in particular. One basis of ecumenical engagement, he said, quoting Pope John Paul II, "lies in our common mutual knowledge of ourselves as men and women who have sinned."

HB Sfeir then turned to a theme that was repeated through all five speeches, that of Christian emigration from the Middle East. "We must stop this continuous bleeding of human resources... the emigration of our children outside their Eastern home." How, he asked, can the Holy Land be emptied of Christians after it had witnessed the birth, life and resurrection of Christ? This question has not been answered.

HB Ignatius IV Hazim, Patriarch of Antioch and all the East, spoke on behalf of the Eastern Orthodox family. Speaking of the early days of the ecumenical movement, he said, "When we met, we met as foreigners. We did not know each other's language, how each of us spoke of themselves or understood themselves... We have gradually overcome our fear of learning from others and started to learn from one another."

Doctrines, Hazim said, cannot separate believers. Those who believe in one God and Creator are united in that faith. Those who were not afraid to meet and make a dialogue have now passed beyond the point where they are stuck with one language.

In recognition of this reality, he said, it was necessary to reinvent the MECC, to help it to be more active than ever. It is not enough that MECC be a council for a few people within the various churches - it must be a council for the many. MECC must address the churches as ecumenical churches and show them something new that they can partake of.

HH Catholicos Aram I of the Armenian Apostolic Church's Great House of Cilicia, representing the Oriental Orthodox family, spoke next. He focussed on the challenges faced by Christians in the Middle East, in a context full of tensions, conflicts, and polarizations. In some countries, Christians do not enjoy the full range of liberties they are due as human beings. There are tremendous difficulties facing the Church in the Middle East, difficulties that make it all the more important to strengthen ecumenical collaboration between the churches.

Aram made a point of using the phrase "Christian witness" rather than "Christian presence" - Christian presence, after all, is and must be a witness for Christ to the world. This witness can be strengthened by ecumenical cooperation in the areas of social diaconia, Christian education, theological formation, common actions toward peace and justice, and theological dialogue on practical issues such as mutual recognition of baptism or agreement on the dates of the major Christian holy days.

Aram mentioned two major concerns facing the Church in the Middle East. The first was migration, which he asserted was not a concept but a fact attested to by the bitter experience of all the clergy present. This emigration is in some cases exacerbated by some Western countries and Western Christian organizations which, for various reasons and due to various motives, have the effect of encouraging emigration.

The second major issue facing the Church in the Middle East according to Aram is the participation of youth in its life and witness. "The younger generation wants a relevant, responsive church. They are facing many concerns and stresses, and they look to the Church for answers. It is up to us to make those concerns a part and parcel of our life and witness, and become a church that makes a difference for our young people."

Aram closed his speech with a pair of other issues upon which he thought it would be fruitful for the churches to focus. One was the age-old dialogue with Islam. There are a number of issues, Aram said, where we can engage in positive common action with our Muslim brothers and sisters. The second was the various diasporas. These churches, although they often provide financial support to the churches in the East, are no less dependent on their family in their native lands for help with spiritual and human resources. The difficulties in maintaining an identity as Middle Eastern Christians outside of the Middle Eastern context are many, and there is a real danger to the diaspora Christians' tradition, identity and faith.

The Revd Dr Salim Sahiouny, President of the Supreme Council of the Evangelical Churches in Syria and Lebanon, spoke on behalf of the Evangelical family. In an address that was more overtly theological where the others had been historical or programmatic, he called on those present to all raise their voices and sing songs of thanks to God, knowing that he has helped the ecumenical movement all the way. After all, "If God is with us, who can be against us?"

Reflecting on the unity of the churches toward which the ecumenical movement is leading, he noted that it need not be an administrative or structural unity, but rather one of visible preaching and service. This "unity in diversity" is at the core of the Christian faith - we believe, after all, in a God who is one God in three persons, and our holy book reflects a unity in its essence despite a diversity in its expressions. He closed by praying that the will of the one Head and Founder of the Church would be realized in the unity of the Church in this place where Jesus was born.

The Revd Dr Riad Jarjour, MECC General Secretary, followed with his address. Vowing to "speak the truth about the state of this crisis-ridden and unprecedented world," he sketched a brief overview of the region's problems. He expressed anguish and support for the people of Palestine, then touched briefly on the situations in the Syrian Golan, South Lebanon, Cyprus and Iraq.

He then turned to the aspirations specific to the region's Christians. Taking up the issue of emigration, he mentioned the urgent need for societies founded upon respect for diversity, the affirmation of full equality among their citizens, and upon upholding human dignity and rights. This, he said, was the only way that the haemorrhage of human resources among the Christians of the region.

He continued by calling for Christian unity and for the strengthening of co-existence among Muslims and Christians, then closed his remarks with a prayer "that God will guide our footsteps toward that which gives Him the glory and benefits our people".

Appendix 4

The Pastoral Letter Issued by the Heads of the Churches of the Middle East at their meeting on 20 and 21 November, 2000 in Bkirke, Lebanon

We praise God the Father whose love binds us by faith in Jesus Christ, in the joy of the Holy Spirit. We, the heads of churches of the four families, Orthodox, Oriental Orthodox, Catholic and Evangelical, meet in Bkirke, the seat of the Antiochene Maronite Patriarchate, hosted by His Beatitude Patriarch Cardinal Mar Nasrallah Boutros Sfeir.

Our biannual meeting this year is distinguished by its occurrence during the celebrations of the second millennium since the birth of our Lord and God Jesus Christ. We are called to take the opportunity of this holy year to examine ourselves before God in meditation, reflection and prayer, so that the occasion shall bring forth new life in our churches, families and societies, and in every single one of us.

We are inspired, as we meet, by the miracle of the multiplying of the loaves (Luke 9:10-17) hoping that, through it, Christ shall give people life and give it abundantly (John 10:10). We meet as Eastern Christians rooted in our land, confident in our future, joyful in our hope, witnessing to our Lord and Saviour, and willing to be those five loaves which, being blessed by the Lord Jesus Christ, fed thousands and "twelve basketfuls ... were left over" (Luke 9:17).

We the Churches of the East are primarily concerned with commemorating the second millennium of the birth of our Lord Jesus Christ, born in a humble place in our land, in Bethlehem. Our forefathers were the first of those who heard the good news and rejoiced in it, accepted it and proclaimed it. Our fathers then struggled to safeguard this legacy as their apostolic heritage, which our churches formulated in the Nicene-Constantinopolitan creed. This creed we unanimously uphold to this day. On this blessed occasion, our eyes and hearts turn to Christ Jesus, the foundation of our faith, the rock of our salvation, who is the same yesterday, today and forever (Hebrews 13:8).

It behoves us today to renew our covenant with Christ and deepen our faith in Him so that the beauty of his face and the majesty of his glory may be visible in our personal lives and those of our families, churches and societies. We are bound to be the truest witnesses to those who ask of us a sign of our hope, in humility and reverence (1 Peter 3:15-16). We do this in a world of conflicting currents, torn by challenges, overwhelmed by changes and governed by the logic of consumerism, opportunism and hedonism.

Since its birth, Christianity in our homeland has interacted with and enriched the civilizations and cultures of the East, exhibiting the wonderful potential of the Gospel to contextualise itself in all human environments. Christianity has formed many traditions with distinctive spiritualities, liturgies and schools of thought; it is rich in its Fathers and its saints.

However, this variety, at certain times in our history, has turned into controversy, and even into conflict and schism. The one Church became separated churches. Elements of alienation and estrangement were compounded. Conflicts arose, driven by differing social and political interests as well as selfishness and opposing desires.

At the outset of the third millennium, we are fully conscious of the need to continue in our efforts towards healing, dialogue and solidarity. This ecumenical endeavour will not achieve its goal unless our churches are renewed in spirit and mind. This spiritual renewal, planted and nurtured in our churches, is the guarantee of their faithfulness on the road to unity.

Our meeting today is nothing other than a sign that our ecumenical commitment is our choice for the present and the future. It is our response to the will of Christ expressed in his prayer for the unity of those who believe in him "That all of them may be one, Father, just as you are in me and I am in you. May they also be in us so that the world may believe that you have sent me." (John 17:21).

We are fully aware that our Christian witness is incomplete as long as we are divided. We know that the road ahead is long and that many difficulties await us. Therefore, as we hear the voice of the master saying "Take courage! It is I. Don't be afraid" (Matthew 14:27), we affirm our commitment to hasten our steps on the path to unity. We have, by the inspiration of the Holy Spirit, made important steps toward rapprochement and friendship between our churches. And by the power of Christ, tangible results have been accomplished which cannot be ignored.

We see in the Middle East Council of Churches a concrete expression of this movement. In it we meet and through it we work together for unity. We are keen to keep the Council active in the churches and viable as a forum where the churches meet. It is our desire that the Council remain close to the everyday life of the churches so that it may not grow old, but stay vibrantly alive and be ever renewed. Pastoral agreements between member churches have been reached, which, if applied, will act to encourage further efforts making our common witness more effective on the global ecumenical level.

In his eternal wisdom, God willed that we be his witnesses in this part of the world. This gives us joy, and we gladly respond to the responsibilities and privileges this entails. Our churches are rooted in this land and situated at the heart of its societies, sharing in the building of the human person and participating in public life in all its facets, requirements, problems and sacrifices. We stand in solidarity with the poor, the needy, the marginalized and the oppressed.

We have discussed the challenges facing Christians today such as emigration, participation in public affairs, and the need to invigorate the role of youth and engage in a positive dialogue with them. We considered the problems posed by the globalisation of culture and the media, and the influence of such globalisation on the awareness of their Christian identity among the youth of our countries, as well as on their values and lifestyles. We reiterate the need to encounter these challenges with objectivity, wisdom and creativity, steering away from exaggerations, fear and threats. This does not mean we should ignore any difficulties. On the contrary, we call upon the faithful to face these challenges without sway and urge them to join hands as they benefit from their various potentialities in pastoral and diaconal work, and to invigorate the role of Christian individuals and institutions for the public good.

Our presence in society is for the sake of the human person who is created by God in his image and likeness, who is loved by God and for whom the Lord Christ was made man, died and rose from the dead. This is the person who God does not forget, and therefore neither can our churches. We struggle to promote every human person's spiritual growth, social progress and national liberation.

We turn to our fellow citizens, the Muslims, with whom we share the same national allegiance to our common land, and the same concerns and destiny. We shall continue to work together in the existential dialogue of life for the sake of a society that respects differences, achieves equality, safeguards freedoms, and protects human rights and dignity. We are encouraged by the good relationship now existing between us and the dialogue initiatives and joint efforts we have engaged in.

Today, as in all similar meetings held by our churches, we renew our commitment to the just causes of our peoples. We first turn our eyes to Palestine, the place of the nativity of the Lord Christ and the land of his incarnation and mission. The continual suffering of the Palestinian people is ever-present in our minds. Today, more than at any other time, they suffer from the oppression of occupation and its violence. Their children are being killed and starved. They live under siege and their lands and possessions are violated. They are simply a people struggling to regain their legitimate rights.

Rockets plant death, they do not make peace. Peace will not prevail unless the full national and human rights of the Palestinian people are recognized; this requires the establishment of an independent Palestinian state with Jerusalem as its capital. This is what international legality has affirmed. Peace shall not come in our region unless all Arab land is returned to its rightful owners, the Golan Heights not excluded.

The recent events in Jerusalem prove that the city cannot be separated from the Palestinian body. It is close to the Palestinian heart and must be returned to its owners so that it may play its authentic role as a city of justice, peace, dialogue and reconciliation, and become a city of peaceful encounter and prayer for all the faithful. In the midst of the ongoing struggle now raging between Palestinians and Israelis, we call upon the faithful of the Jewish religion that they may also contribute through their faith to the establishment of the justice and truth called for by Palestinians.

We share the struggles and hopes of the Lebanese people of all confessional groups. We rejoice in the liberation of its South from Israeli occupation. We look forward to the return of all land still occupied and hope for the full restoration of Lebanon's independence, sovereignty and freedom of decision, for its economic recovery, for communal reconciliation between its inhabitants and the unity of its people, and for the preservation of the rights and freedoms of its citizens. All this must take place for Lebanon to resume its leadership role for the welfare of the whole region.

We hold up the tragedy of the Iraqi people after ten years of collective punishment. The misery they endure has reached unbearable levels, and cannot be accepted by any living human conscience. We lift our voices high before the whole world for the sake of the Iraqi people, so that the yoke of the unjust siege may be lifted from their children, their youth, their elderly and their whole people.

We also remember the right of the Cypriot people to a peace based on justice. We support its continuous effort, since the occupation of the island in 1974, to recover the unity of its land and people. This unity must include the return of all refugees to their homes and the retrieval of their property, and must proceed by way of negotiations under the auspices of the United Nations, guaranteeing the human rights of all Cyprus's inhabitants.

Dear brothers, sisters and beloved children,
At the dawn of the third millennium, our churches stand together in faith, hope, love and joy, having full trust in the Lord Christ who gives us life and is with us and in us for all times and unto ages of ages. Amen.

Appendix 5

Common Easter Message by Their Beatitudes the Patriarchs and Their Excellencies the Heads of the Churches of Jerusalem

"Christ is risen" (Luke 24:1-52).

Jesus, Lord and Saviour, has risen today, just as He had foretold His apostles. "They will put Him to death, and on the third day He will rise again." (Matthew 17:23).

Indeed, after the suffering and death of our Lord Jesus Christ, the Churches of Jerusalem witness with one voice and one heart to the glory of His Resurrection as they rejoice in the hope and strength that comes from that empty tomb in the heart of our Holy City.

Before bearing the cross Himself, Jesus had called upon His disciples to carry the cross and follow Him. He had asked them to walk the narrow path that leads toward salvation. This double vision of the cross and the Resurrection applies to the situation in which we find ourselves today.

Our suffering and fear in the past few months has increased in view of the uncertainty of the political situation. We reassure each and every one of our sons and daughters that we share the pain of every family that is deprived of hope as they go through their daily lives without jobs and income or are exposed physically and psychologically to the painful measures that are imposed upon them.

Although the closures that are sealing most of the Palestinian territories bring days of deep despair, we ought to remain committed to hope. "I call heaven and earth to witness against you today that I have set before you life and death, blessing and curses. Choose life so that you and your descendants may live."(Deuteronomy 30:19).

In this cycle of struggle and suffering, we detect also the way of the cross that will ultimately lead toward the glory of the Resurrection. Thus celebrating Easter means the restoration of our hope that victory of life over death also will be witnessed in the troubled land of ours.

This will only happen when violence and discrimination give way for a real peace, between the "two peoples and the three religions" of this small land where God chose to reveal His divine will. Such a peace can only be secured through mutual reconciliation based on the respect for the dignity and value God has given to all human beings.

In no way can this peace be imposed by sheer force: it is nurtured by an honest application of justice and mercy in line with internationally accepted legitimate resolutions for the benefit of the weaker part.

Therefore, all of us, who claim faith in the Living God who has overcome death and sin, are called today to witness and work with steadfast determination and persistent commitment. The words of the prophet Isaiah come fittingly to mind: "See the former things have come to pass and new things I now declare: before they spring forth I tell you of them."(Isaiah 42:9)

God speaks to us of a time in which the relationship of creation with the Creator is restored, justice is the benchmark of every nation, and the light of redemption shines in the deepest corners of despair.

As all the Churches of Jerusalem celebrate the paschal festivities together this first year of the new millennium, they also affirm that the experience of Easter is one of liberation. It is a triumph of life over death, of peace over violence. Looking at the One God who manifested His power over servitude and death, we address all secular and political authorities to welcome into their hearts the good will and good faith that builds new generations with renewed hope and sustained confidence.

Today, we ask our faithful in the Holy Land as well as all believers world-wide to share with us in the transformation of hearts and minds so that the true joy that comes with the Risen Lord can also infuse their own lives.

We pray for an end to the unjustifiable deaths that plague our societies. We pray for the immediate end of all collective punishments, especially for the lifting of the closures of Palestinians towns and villages. We pray for the good will of Palestinians and Israelis, of

Jews, Christians and Muslims alike in actively working for justice and peace. We pray for equality so that one no longer sees the neighbour as an enemy but rather as a brother or sister with whom to build a new society.

Ours is a message of hope and compassion, of reconciliation and joy. To all, we affirm that Easter is the time to become one voice and one heart before the Lord so that "we may come to know Him and the power of the Resurrection" (Philippians 3:10) in a genuine, just and comprehensive peace that no longer disparages one God-given life over another.

Our Christian message remains constant year in year out. Life conquers death, and love defeats hatred. Hope tramples desolation, joy overcomes despair and peace ends violence. So let us all proclaim together: "Where, O death, is your victory? Where, O death, is your sting?.. But thanks to God, who gives us the victory through our Lord Jesus Christ". (1Corinthians 15:55.57).

The Lord is risen! He is risen indeed.

Signed by the Heads of the thirteen traditional Churches in Jerusalem:

+	Metropolitan Cornelius:	Locum Tenens, Greek Orthodox Patriarchate
+	Patriarch Michel Sabbah:	Latin Patriarchate
+	Patriarch Torkom II:	Armenian Apostolic Orthodox Patriarchate
+	Ignatius VIII Pierre Abdul-Ahad:	Syrian Catholic Patriarch
	Father Giovanni Battistelli:	Latin Catholic Custos of the Holy Land
+	Anba Abraham:	Coptic Orthodox Patriarchate
+	Sewerios Malki Mourad:	Syrian Orthodox Patriarchate
+	Abba Gabriel:	Ethiopian Orthodox Patriarchate
+	Riah Abu Al-Assal:	Episcopal Church of Jerusalem & the Middle East
+	Mounib Younan:	Evangelical Lutheran Church
+	Maximus Sallum:	Greek Catholic (Melkite) Patriarchal Exarchate
+	Paul Nabil Sayyah:	Maronite Patriarchal Exarchate
+	Andrea Dikran Bedoghlyan:	Armenian Catholic Patriarchal Exarcate

Easter   2001

Appendix 6

Speech given in the Abu Nour Mosque, Damascus, by the Very Revd Dr Robert Davidson, Former Moderator, General Assembly of the Church of Scotland 16 March 2001

On behalf of the delegation from the Churches Together in Britain and Ireland, may I thank Grand Mufti Khuftaro for his gracious willingness to allow this ecumenical message to be delivered. It is a very real privilege to be here today in this world-famous Mosque. In this place across many centuries, thanks to the skill and devotion of architects, builders, craftsmen and artists, the faithful have been filled with a sense of the greatness and the presence of God.

Five of us have been in Beirut and are today in Damascus. Four of our colleagues have visited Cairo and are now in Amman. Three others are on their way from Beirut to Amman, where we will meet them tonight. Our Middle East journeys could not have been undertaken without the willing assistance of the Middle East Council of Churches, whose partnership we value highly.

We have all come to the Middle East from different Church traditions, but we have been learning in recent years to grow closer together, recognizing the faith we hold in common beyond our divisions. I believe the same can, and ought to be true, in relationships between Muslims and Christians. I have seen it happening in Scotland, in the city of Glasgow from which I come. There is a significant Muslim community in the city. My children went to a primary school in which over 80 per cent of the pupils came from that community. They were well grounded at school in the significance of Islamic festivals. Indeed, there were times when I began to wonder whether my children knew more about Islam than about Christianity. A splendid mosque was built which, as far as being an appropriate centre for worship was concerned, was the envy of many Christians. Groups from churches were encouraged to visit the mosque, and were always warmly welcomed. During the Gulf War, leaders from the churches and from the mosque met and together publicly protested against misunderstandings of Islam which were circulating. These meetings have continued across the years leading to growing mutual understanding. Together we share a faith which has its roots in Abraham, a faith which unites us as fellow believers in the one God who is compassionate and merciful.

Sadly this has not always been so. I need not remind you of age-old, violent distortions of the Christian faith - nor of the ways in which, down to the present day, forcible conversions have taken place and conflicts arisen between Muslim and Christian communities, conflicts often instigated by political tensions which have little to do with the religions we confess. Offensive caricatures of Islam still regrettably appear in the more irresponsible media in the West.

Yes, there are differences between Christians and Muslims -- in what we believe and in our life styles, differences which we should neither attempt to ignore or to conceal. Indeed I believe that future relations depend upon our being honest about such differences and respecting each other's right to be different. Only then can there be a true basis for continuing dialogue, a dialogue which should drive us all back to explore the beating heart of what we believe, and challenge us to live as we are commanded to live in response to the faith we confess. We are conscious of and give thanks for the courageous part which the Grand Mufti himself has played in pioneering dialogue between people of different faiths.

Nowhere is such dialogue more vital than in the troubled world of the Middle East today, where there is a desperate need for that peace with justice for which so many Muslims, Christians and Jews yearn. Let us be clear that there will be no lasting peace between nations, unless there is peace between religions.

I am reliably informed that one of the questions Palestinians are sometimes asked when they come to an Israeli checkpoint on the road between Bethlehem and Jerusalem, is "Are you a Christian or a Muslim?". This is a question Israelis have no right to ask at a military checkpoint. It is being asked in an attempt to drive a wedge between Christians and Muslims in Palestine by sowing the seeds of suspicion that one religious community will be treated with greater respect than the other. But today in Palestine Christians and Muslims face the same frustrations, the same denial of human rights. Their casualties are treated in the same hospitals. In countless ways they seek to support each other in the face of the hardships, the pain and the grief they endure. Once peace and security return to the land, there will be a humbling and encouraging story to be told of inter faith sharing. And not only between Christians and Muslims.

Listen to these wise words:

"When war is called peace, when oppression and persecution are referred to as security, and assassination is called liberation, the defilement of language proceeds and prepares the way for the defilement of life and dignity."

These are the words of a Jewish writer protesting against the disinformation and indeed the lies which were being fed to his people to justify the Israeli invasion of Lebanon in 1982, and the tragic consequences which ensued.

Surely we are all committed to protest against such defilement of life and human dignity wherever it occurs, and on whomsoever's lips such words appear.

Let me close by reminding you of words which speak to all of us from the Psalms of David:

"Though the Lord is high, he regards the lowly,
but the haughty he perceives from afar.
Though I walk in the midst of trouble,
you preserve me against the wrath of my enemies;
you stretch out your hand,
and your right hand delivers me."

In that faith and with that assurance let us pledge ourselves to walk together along a road of hope which will lead to that world of peace, justice and security which today so many people do not have, but for which they and we yearn so deeply.

Appendix 7

Appeal of Jerusalem Church Leaders, 24 March 2001

We the Heads of Churches in Jerusalem: -

.....concerned for the spiritual, mental and bodily well-being of all the citizens of this Holy Land, Christian, Moslem and Jew, appeal to the Israeli Government, the Palestinian Authority; World Leaders (Secular and Religious); as well as to all men and women of goodwill to help bring an urgent conclusion to the conflict affecting the lives of thousands in this Land.

We are convinced that peace-seeking negotiations between the Israelis and the Palestinians are the only assured way of providing for the well being of all our peoples.

We believe that the violence which has intensified over these past months will only end when both parties in the conflict make a determined effort to respect each other's rights whilst affirming the dignity and worth of every human life (man, woman and child).

We would respectfully request protection for all our people in order to assist the re-establishment of mutual trust and security for Israeli and Palestinian. Further we would call on all peace-loving people from around the world to come and join us in a manifestation of just peace.

Furthermore, we would ask for even greater assistance from our brothers and sisters abroad — Governments, Aid Agencies as well as Churches and private individuals —for those in need in the areas of conflict. Despite all the kind help to date (for which we express sincere gratitude) many are desperate for food, clothing, shelter and the like. In this appeal for help we would call to mind the words of Jesus when He said "In as much as you do this for the least of these my little ones, you do it for me". (Matthew 25:40)

In a few weeks all the Christians of the world will celebrate together the commemoration of the Death and Resurrection of Jesus Christ Jesus died to offer the world God's forgiveness and encourage reconciliation. He rose again to offer the world fullness of life. We firmly believe that now is the time to establish forgiveness and reconciliation on all sides in order to work for fullness of life for every citizen of this Land.

Jerusalem
24 March 2001

Appendix 8 - The Middle East - at a glance
Lebanon
Area: 10,452 sq km   GNP: US $15.9 billion
Capital: Beirut   GNP per head: US $3,720
Population: 3.5 million   Average Annual Growth per head: +0.5%
Language: Arabic (official), French, English, Armenian
People: Arabs (95%), Armenians (4%), Palestinians, Kurds and others (1%), Religious groups: Muslim (60%) – 5 legally recognized: Shia, Sunni, Druze, Ismailite and Alawite. Christian (40%) – 11 legally recognized groupings: 4 Orthodox, 6 Catholic and 1 Protestant.

Israel and Palestine*
Area: 26,990 sq km   GNP: US $96.5 billion
(6220 sq km in Gaza & West Bank) GNP per head: US $16,180
Capital: Tel Aviv   Average Annual Growth per head: +1.2%
Population: 8.5 million *(5.8m in Israel; 2.7m in Gaza & West Bank)*
Language: Hebrew, Arabic, English
People: Jewish (81.4%), Arabs and others (18.6%) Religious groups: Israel – Judaism (80.1%), Muslim, mostly Sunni (14.6%), Christians (2.1%) and others (3.2%); Palestine – Muslim, mostly Sunni (75%), Jewish (17%), Christians and others (8%)

Syria
Area: 185,180 sq km   GNP: US $16 billion
Capital: Damascus   GNP per head: US $1,010
Population: 17 million   Average Annual Growth per head: -1.4%
Language: Arabic, Kurdish, Armenian, Turkish, English
People: Arabs (90%), Kurds, Armenian, Circassians, Turks Religious groups: Sunni Muslim (74%), other Muslim (16%), Christian (10%)

Egypt
Area: 1,001,449 sq km   GNP: US $86.5 billion
Capital: Cairo   GNP per head: US $1,390
Population: 67 million   Average Annual Growth per head: +3.8%
Language: Arabic
People: Berbers, Bedouins and Egyptians (99%), others (1%) Religious groups: Islam, mostly Sunni (90%), Christian (7%)

Jordan
Area: 89,206 sq km   GNP: US $6.7 billion
Capital: Amman   GNP per head: US $1,430
Population: 4.6 million   Average Annual Growth per head: +1%
Language: Arabic, English
People: Arabs (total 98% - 60% Palestinians, many refugees) Religious groups: Sunni Muslim (96%), Christian (4%)

*Source: World Bank 1999   *World Bank 1998*